USS Charger
CVE-30

Bryan J. Dickerson

DEDICATION

To Andrew S. Futey, Ralph Thibodeau, and all who served aboard *USS Charger* during her service to our nation in World War Two.

CONTENTS

	Acknowledgments	i
	Introduction	ii
1	The Need for Escort Carriers	Pg 1
2	Sun Shipbuilding	Pg 16
3	*USS Charger*	Pg 20
4	Operation Torch	Pg 29
5	After Torch	Pg 45
6	ENS Ralph A. Thibodeau	Pg 75
7	Andrew S. Futey	Pg 80
8	Mishaps	Pg 85
9	*USS Charger* in 1944	Pg 87
10	Life Aboard Ship	Pg 112
11	The Last Year of the War	Pg 114
12	*Charger* After the War	Pg 132
13	*Charger*'s Sailors and Pilots After the War	Pg 135
	Conclusion	Pg 141
	Charger Photo Album	Pg 142
	Appendixes	Pg 153
	Sources	Pg 165

ACKNOWLEDGMENTS

The Author wishes to thank Ralph Thibodeau Jr., Paul Trangmar, and the National Archives for their assistance with this book. The Author also thanks the U.S. Naval History and Heritage Command for the use of several of their photos for this book.

INTRODUCTION

She never engaged in any battles. Her aircraft never sank or even damaged any enemy ships. Except for two brief forays, she never ventured from the confines of the Chesapeake Bay. Yet, the escort carrier *USS Charger* (CVE-30) contributed significantly to the defeat of the Axis Powers. US Navy and British Royal Navy pilots that trained upon her flight deck went on to defeat the Imperial Japanese Navy in the Pacific and wrest control of the Atlantic Ocean from the German U-Boats.

Some of my earliest childhood memories are of my grandfather - Andrew Steve Futey - telling stories of his service in the United States Navy during World War Two. He only served aboard one ship - a small training aircraft carrier named *USS Charger.* I would hang on his every word as he described life aboard ship, working in the engine room and watching pilots practicing their landings -- and not always being successful. He was proud of his time in the Navy. My grandfather passed away in October 2001 but it wasn't until this year that I had the opportunity to write about his ship. This paper is mostly based upon official Navy records kept in the National Archives, and my grandfather's personnel records and is supplemented by several other primary and secondary sources. It is my tribute to my dearly departed grandfather and all those who served aboard this small but important aircraft carrier in World War Two.

Chapter One
The Need for Escort Carriers

The escort aircraft carrier was born out of necessity in the midst of a raging battle for control of the Atlantic Ocean during World War Two.

The Development of the Aircraft Carrier

Between the Wright Brothers first powered flight in December 1903 and the end of the First World War in November 1918, aviation progressed at an astonishing pace.   One of those developments was the launching and landing of aircraft from ships. Thus came to be the aircraft carrier, at first a novelty but ultimately, one of the most dominant weapons systems ever employed.

In the years that followed World War One, the aircraft carrier developed from a novel concept into a viable weapons system. Britain, Japan and the United States were the primary naval powers that operated carriers before the start of World War Two.   The

Washington Naval Treaty of 1922 limited but could not stop the development of aircraft carriers.[1]

America's first aircraft carrier was *USS Langley* (CV-1), which was basically the collier *Jupiter* reconstructed with a flat flight deck over her hull, a hangar deck to store aircraft and a new name. She entered service in 1922 and served as a test platform to develop and refine carrier operational methods. *Langley* was followed by two large carriers - *Lexington* (CV-2) and *Saratoga* (CV-3) - that had been constructed on the hulls of incomplete battle cruisers. *USS Ranger* (CV-4) was America's first carrier built from the keel up specifically as an aircraft carrier. At 14,500 tons displacement, she was significantly smaller than *Lexington* and *Saratoga*. *Ranger* was followed by two much larger carriers, *Yorktown* (CV-5) and *Enterprise* (CV-6). The next carrier, *Wasp* (CV-7) was similar in size to *Ranger.* She was followed by *Hornet* (CV-8) which was built like *Yorktown* and *Enterprise.*

The Battle of the Atlantic

World War Two did not begin well for Great Britain and the Allied Powers. The first two years of the war saw Nazi Germany seize Poland, the Low Countries, France, Norway, the Balkans, and large sections of North Africa and the Soviet Union in rapid succession. At sea, German warships and submarines (U-Boats) wreaked havoc upon Britain's sea commerce; the hard-pressed Royal Navy was losing in the struggle to keep Britain's sea lanes open. By 1941, Britain was practically waging war against Nazi Germany in

---

[1] For more about the development of aircraft carriers, see Scot MacDonald, *Evolution of Aircraft Carriers.* (Washington DC GPO: Office of the Chief of Naval Operations, 1962), pp. 49-53.; and Donald Macintyre, *Aircraft Carrier: The Majestic Weapon.* (NY: Ballantine Books, 1968).

the West alone.   In the Pacific, Japan had been aggressively expanding in China for several years and was planning further expansion into southeast Asia and Indonesia.

When World War Two began in September 1939, the aircraft carrier was barely twenty years old.   Even at this date, the idea of launching and recovering aircraft from a ship underway at sea was still a controversial and revolutionary concept. The prevailing naval strategies of the day involved climactic surface engagements between battleships and cruisers.   But the winds of naval aviation change were blowing with increasing intensity.

From the beginning of the war, the British battled against the German Navy in the Atlantic Ocean to keep open its vital sea lanes to cargo ships. As the Germans were able to devote more resources to the Battle of the Atlantic, the British found it more and more difficult to protect its vital shipping from destruction. The German Kriegsmarine utilized U-Boats (submarines), surface raiders and aircraft in an attempt to strangle Britain's sea lifelines. The Kriegsmarine's surface fleet was far smaller than the German High Seas Fleet of the First World War.   Unable to confront the Royal Navy on anything approaching equal terms, the Kriegsmarine instead used their surface ships for commerce raiding. Like the First World War, German naval strategy employed submarines against Britain's sea lanes.   Shore-based German aircraft posed an additional threat to British maritime operations through reconnaissance and by attacking merchant ships.

Though lacking the numbers to engage the Royal Navy head on, the Kriegsmarine did possess several powerful warships capable of inflicting major destruction upon British merchant shipping and

British warships in isolated engagements. The pocket battleship (Panzerschiff) *Admiral Graf Spee* sank or captured nine ships before being engaged by three British cruisers in the Battle of the River Plate off Uruguay in late December 1939. Severely damaged and unable to escape, her captain scuttled her. A year and a half later, the battleship *Bismarck* and the heavy cruiser *Prinz Eugen* broke into the Atlantic Ocean. In her first surface engagement, *Bismarck* sank the pride of the Royal Navy - the battlecruiser *HMS Hood*. The new British battleship *HMS Prince of Wales* was also damaged in the engagement. Infuriated by the loss of *Hood* with all hands, the Royal Navy mobilized all available naval resources to find and sink *Bismarck*. A fortuitous hit by a Fairey Swordfish torpedo plane jammed *Bismarck*'s rudder and enabled pursuing British battleships and cruisers to catch up with the German behemoth and send her to the bottom of the Atlantic.

At Adolf Hitler's insistence, the German naval strategy was switched in its emphasis from surface warships and raiders to U-Boats. German U-Boats were not true submarines in that they required considerable time on the surface to re-charge their electric batteries for submerged operation. Nevertheless, their mobility and their ability to strike from below without warning devastated British shipping in the Atlantic Ocean.

Depending upon where they were sailing, convoys also had to contend with German land-based aircraft. In the Mediterranean Sea especially, convoys came under frequent air attack. Escort vessels and cargo ships alike suffered heavily under these attacks.

In response to German naval threats, Britain quickly adopted the convoy system that had worked so well against German U-Boats in World War One. Early in the war, the British with the assistance of Polish military intelligence were able to break the German Enigma codes, thus gaining a highly valuable resource against the U-Boats. Unfortunately, Britain lacked adequate numbers of escort vessels to protect its convoys. Nor could code-breaking alone ensure the destruction of the U-Boats and the survival of the convoys. Aircraft were highly effective against the U-Boats but land-based aircraft could not adequately cover the entire routes taken by convoys. In response, German naval leadership simply moved their U-Boats beyond the range of the land-based aircraft. This area became known as the "Black Gap."

As 1941 progressed, the United States became closer and closer to entering the Battle of Atlantic. Woefully unprepared for war, the United States embarked upon a crash program to modernize and expand its military and naval forces. The shipbuilding program for FY1941 represented new warship construction that greatly surpassed the preceding ten years of warship construction combined. U.S. Navy warships began escorting convoys part of the way across the Atlantic. To help Britain with its escort ship shortage, President Franklin D. Roosevelt traded fifty World War One-era destroyers for basing rights in the Caribbean.

The greater role played by the U.S. Navy in escorting trans-Atlantic convoys helped the British in contending with the U-Boat but it did not solve the problem of major gaps in air coverage for convoys.

The United States Entered the War

By the end of 1941, the United States was essentially fighting an undeclared naval war against Nazi Germany in the Atlantic. Already, fire had been exchanged between U.S. Navy warships and German U-Boats. So essentially the United States was unofficially in the war against Nazi Germany months before it was officially in the war.

The United States entered World War Two when the Japanese launched air strikes from six of its carriers against the US Pacific Fleet's base at Pearl Harbor, Hawaii. The air strikes inflicted much destruction upon the fleet, and in particular its battleships. Fortunately all three of the US Pacific Fleet carriers were not at Pearl Harbor and thus avoided destruction.

The entry of the United States into the war against Nazi Germany actually made the situation in the Atlantic worse than before. The U.S. entry into the war eliminated all restraints for German submarine warfare. The United States was completely unprepared to counter the U-Boat threat, especially off its East and Gulf Coasts. With just a handful of U-Boats, the Germans were able to inflict a tremendous amount of destruction on Allied shipping in those first awful few months...right up to the very shoreline of the United States. Ships were being sunk by U-Boats within sight of the American mainland.

After a few devastating months, the U.S. Navy and the U.S. Army Air Force was able to work out a system to convoy ships in the coastal shipping lanes, and use aircraft and ship patrols to counter U-Boats. The Kriegsmarine adapted to the increased U.S. anti-submarine efforts by pulling the U-Boats farther east into the Atlantic to reduce the effectiveness of air patrols.

Introduction of Escort Carriers

With U-Boats operating successfully farther from American air bases, the problem of the mid-Atlantic air gap, ie. 'the Black Gap' re-emerged. To better protect its convoys and to destroy the U-Boat threat, the Allies needed a way to project air power across the entire Atlantic Ocean.

A solution to the convoy protection and air support problems began to emerge in the form of the escort aircraft carrier. The escort aircraft carrier was thus created to eliminate the 'Black Gap,' better protect the convoys, and destroy the U-Boat threat.

Basically, the escort carrier was a small aircraft carrier constructed on the hull of a merchant ship and equipped with a small complement of aircraft --- very similar indeed to America's first aircraft carrier *Langley*. The concept of the escort aircraft carrier or light aircraft carrier had been advanced as early as the closing days of World War One. In May 1927, U.S. Navy Lieutenant Commander Bruce G. Leighton wrote a paper on the subject which would later prove prescient. The idea was brought again to the forefront in 1939. Support for the concept was mixed in the U.S. Navy. In 1940, Rear Admiral William F. Halsey and Admiral Husband Kimmel both supported the concept as a way to free up the fleet aircraft carriers from having to ferry aircraft from the United States to distant U.S. bases overseas.[2]

President Roosevelt ultimately decided the issue in October of 1940. By now, the plan was to take existing merchant ships and convert them to small aircraft carriers by the installation of a flight deck, hangar facilities and equipment to operate aircraft. Once converted, the escort carriers would escort convoys. Their aircraft would seek out and destroy German U-Boats and surface warships and defend the convoys from air attack. Consultations were held with the U.S. Maritime Commission and arrangements made to acquire merchant ships for the conversion. Additional ships would be acquired by the U.S. Navy, converted to escort carriers, and turned over to the Royal Navy. The Royal Navy was anxious for escort carriers to protect its convoys from U-Boats.[3]

Escort carriers escorted convoys, provided air support for amphibious operations, ferried aircraft for carrier-based and land-based squadrons, and hunted down enemy submarines. Their service during the Battle of the Atlantic proved vital in wresting control of the ocean from German U-Boats. Due to wartime expediency, the CVEs were constructed on the hulls of former merchant ships and tankers. The Sun Shipbuilding and Dry Dock

---

[2] Scot MacDonald. *Evolution of Aircraft Carriers.* (Washington DC GPO: Office of the Chief of Naval Operations, 1962), pp. 49-50. Found online at www.history.navy.mil ; For more about the early development of aircraft carriers, see Captain Donald McIntyre, RN (Ret.), *Aircraft Carrier – The Majestic Weapon.* (NY: Ballantine, 1968.); Samuel Eliot Morison, *History of United States Naval Operations in World War II. Volume. X The Atlantic Battle Won May 1943 – May 1945.* (Boston: Brown, Little & Co., 1956), pp. 37-38. [Hereafter cited as Morison, *The Atlantic Battle Won*].

[3] Ibid.

Company of Chester, Pennsylvania played an important role in producing escort carriers during World War Two. Eight merchant ships constructed at Sun Shipbuilding were purchased by the U.S. Navy and converted to escort carriers for the U.S. and Royal Navies. Altogether, 78 escort carriers were converted from merchant ships or constructed during World War Two.[4]

In March 1941, the U.S. Navy acquired two diesel-powered C-3 cargo ships – *Mormacmail* and *Mormacland* – for conversion to escort carriers. These two vessels had originally been constructed by Sun Shipbuilding for the U.S. Maritime Commission for the Moore-McCormack Shipping Line. The *Mormacmail* became the U.S. Navy's first escort carrier, *USS Long Island* (AVG-1), on 2 June 1941; *Mormacland* was converted and transferred to the Royal Navy as *HMS Archer* (BAVG-1) (D78) the following November.[5]

The U.S. Navy's first escort carrier began life as the C-3 cargo ship *Mormacmail* (Sun Hull Number 185). She was laid down at Sun Shipbuilding on 1 August 1939 along with her sister ship

––––––––––––––––––

[4] The U.S. Navy website provides a brief history of escort carriers. See www.navy.mil/navydata/navy_legacy_hr.asp?id=3 . See also Scot Macdonald's *Evolution of Aircraft Carriers,* and the Sun Ship Historical Society website www.sunshlp.org; CE1 Robert A. Germinsky, USNR. "A Brief History of U.S. Navy Aircraft Carriers - The Escort Carriers." 15 June 2009. Accessed online on 21 April 2020 at https://www.navy.mil/navydata/nav_legacy.asp?id=3

[5] MacDonald, p. 50.; See also the entry for *USS Long Island* in the Dictionary of American Naval Fighting Ships. Hereafter cited as DANFS., McIntyre, p. 119.; Morison, *The Atlantic Battle Won*, p. 38.; Tony Drury has an outstanding website detailing all Royal Navy escort carriers: http://www.royalnavyresearcharchive.org.uk/ESCORT/ . Hereafter this website is cited as "Royal Navy Escort Carriers." My thanks to him for using his website as source material for this paper.

Mormacland. She was launched on 11 January 1940; Mrs. Diane B. Holt was her sponsor. When completed, she was 465 feet in length, with a beam of 69 feet 6 inches and displacing 11,905 tons. Four diesel engines turned a single screw to propel her at 16.5 knots.[6]

The U.S. Navy acquired *Mormacmail* on 6 March 1941 and converted her into an escort carrier. A flight deck, aircraft elevator, hangar and three deck guns were installed. After conversion at Newport News Shipbuilding, the ship displaced 13,499 tons and could operate up to 21 aircraft. Re-named *USS Long Island* (AVG-1), the escort carrier was commissioned on 2 June 1941 under the command of Commander Donald B. Duncan.[7]

In many ways, *USS Long Island* served as the pioneer for the Navy's escort carrier force. Operations quickly revealed that her flight deck was not large enough and so it was expanded. Tests conducted on her enabled to the Navy to develop escort carrier operational doctrine and to make improvements in the design of subsequent carriers. One of those improvements was the addition of an island structure for ship and air operations command and control which *Long Island* lacked.[8]

The U.S. Navy's next acquisitions from Sun Shipbuilding's merchant ship stocks were the four passenger/cargo ships of the *Rio*-class. Named *Rio Hudsun, Rio Pazana, Rio de la Plata* and

---

[6] "Sun Ship Hull Listing."; DANFS.

[7] DANFS.; McIntyre, p.119.; John Moore, Captain, Royal Navy. *Jane's American Fighting Ships of the 20th Century.* (NY: Mallard P, 1991), p. 96.

[8] DANFS.

Rio de Janeiro for rivers in South America, these four ships were in the process of construction when they were acquired by the Navy. Like *Mormacmail* and *Mormacland*, the *Rio* ships were under contract with the U.S. Maritime Commission for the Moore-McCormack Line. Originally they had been intended to transport cargo and passengers between the East Coast of the United States and South America for the Moore-McCormack Line.[9]

After conversion, the four *Rio* escort carriers were transferred to the Royal Navy as *HMS Avenger* (BAVG-2) (D14), *HMS Biter (BAVG-3) (D97), HMS Dasher* (BAVG-5) (D37), and *HMS Charger* (BAVG-4) (AVG-30) (CVE-30). The first three served with distinction in the Royal Navy; *Charger* was re-claimed by the U.S. Navy and used as a training ship.[10]

The last two Sun Shipbuilding ships to be acquired and converted to escort carriers were the *Esso Seakay* and *Esso New Orleans*. These two ships were originally constructed for the U.S. Navy as *Cimarron*-class fast fleet oilers. Two other *Cimarron*-class oilers constructed by another shipbuilder were also acquired. These oilers were chosen because of their larger size and more powerful and reliable engines. *Esso Seakay* became *USS Santee* (CVE-29) and *Esso New Orleans* became *USS Chenango* (CVE-28). Due to the pressing need for fast oilers to support increasing fleet operations, no more *Cimarron* oilers were converted to escort carriers. *Santee* and *Chenango* both conducted operations in the

---

[9] "Sun Ship Hull Listing."; McIntyre, p. 119.; "Royal Navy Escort Carriers."

[10] Ibid.; For *Charger's* history, see DANFS entry.

Atlantic and Pacific Oceans.[11]

The Royal Navy and U.S. Navy escort carriers conducted operations throughout the Atlantic, Pacific and Mediterranean Theaters. In his *First Report to the Secretary of the Navy* issued on 23 April 1944, Fleet Admiral Ernest J. King, USN, described the purpose and utility of the escort carriers. He wrote:

> The "baby flat-tops" have three principal uses. They serve as antisubmarine escorts for convoys; as aircraft transports, delivering assembled aircraft to strategic areas; as combatant carriers to supplement the main air striking force of the fleet. Although their cruising speeds are lower than those of our first-line carriers, these auxiliary carriers can be turned out more rapidly and at a fraction of the cost of conventional carriers. These ships have proved invaluable in performing convoy escort and other duties for which larger and faster carriers are not needed.

In addition to escorting convoys and ferrying aircraft to Allied bases, the "baby flattops" hunted down U-Boats, and supported amphibious invasions.[12]

In November 1942, six of the eight Sun Shipbuilding escort carriers supported Operation Torch – the invasion of North Africa. *Santee, HMS Avenger, HMS Biter,* and *HMS Dasher* provided air

---

[11] "Sun Shipbuilding Hull List."; MacDonald, pp.50-51.; See also DANFS entries for *Santee* and *Chenango.*; McIntyre, p. 120.; Captain John Moore, RN, *Jane's American Fighting Ships of the 20th Century,* p.97.

[12] U.S. Navy. United States Fleet. Commander in Chief, United States Fleet, and Chief of Naval Operations. Fleet Admiral Ernest J. King, USN. *First Report to the Secretary of the Navy.* 23 April 1944. Accessed on 17 April 2020 at http://www.ibiblio.org/hyperwar/USN/USNatWar/USN-King-1.html

cover for the assault forces until land-based aircraft could be established on airfields ashore. *HMS Archer* escorted a U.S. troop convoy and *Chenango* ferried U.S. Army Air Force fighters to the invasion area. In addition, *Charger* ferried U.S. Navy fighter squadron VGF-29 from Norfolk to Bermuda where they transferred to *Santee* for the invasion. Only *Long Island* was not somehow involved in Torch.[13]

Escort carriers did not just escort convoys across the Atlantic Ocean. In 1943, the U.S. Navy formed U-Boat 'hunter-killer' groups consisting of an escort carrier and several destroyers and destroyer-escorts. This lethal combination sought out and destroyed numerous U-Boats. Their task was greatly aided by Allied code-breaking efforts which significantly narrowed the areas of the Atlantic Ocean that needed to be searched for the elusive and deadly foe.[14]

First designated as AVG (Aircraft Escort Vessels) and ACV (Auxiliary Aircraft Carrier), these vital ships eventually came to be officially designated as CVE or Aircraft Carrier Escort. Unofficially, the CVEs were known as "jeep carriers" or the less flattering "Combustible, Vulnerable and Expendable."[15]

---

[13] McIntyre, p. 120.; Samuel Eliot Morison, *History of United States Naval Operations in World War II. Volume. II Operations in North African Waters October 1942 to June 1943.* (Boston: Brown, Little & Co., 1984.), pp. 36-37, 43-44, 118-119, 139, 150-155, 190, 223. [Hereafter cited as Morison, *Operations in North African Waters*].; "Royal Navy Escort Carriers."

[14] CE1 Robert A. Germinsky, USNR. "A Brief History of U.S. Navy Aircraft Carriers - The Escort Carriers."

[15] CE1 Robert A. Germinsky, USNR. "A Brief History of U.S. Navy Aircraft Carriers - The Escort Carriers."

Perhaps the CVEs greatest hour occurred on 25 October 1944 during the Battle off Samar. While covering the invasion forces for the liberation of the Philippines, Task Group 77.4 was attacked by four battleships and six heavy cruisers of the Imperial Japanese Navy under Admiral Takeo Kurita. Kurita's force included the super battleship *Yamato*. TG 77.4 consisted of sixteen "Jeep Carriers" organized into three task units, designated as Taffy 1, Taffy 2, and Taffy 3. Taffy 3 bore the brunt of the surprise Japanese assault. Despite being heavily outgunned, the Taffy 3 escort carriers, destroyers and destroyer escorts put up one of the most valiant fights in naval history. Aircraft from Taffy 1 and Taffy 2 also participated. In the ensuing melee, the escort carrier *USS Gambier Bay* (CVE-73) was sunk along with four destroyers. The ferocity of the American defense convinced Admiral Kurita to abandon his ambitious attack and saved the American invasion forces. After Admiral Kurita turned his forces around, the American task group was subjected to fierce kamikaze attacks, which sank *USS St. Lo* (CVE-63).

Ultimately the United States converted and/or constructed seventy-eight escort carriers, not counting the several that were transferred to the Royal Navy. Of these seventy-eight 'jeep carriers' that served in the U.S. Navy, six were sunk due to enemy action. One was torpedoed by a Japanese submarine. One was sunk by naval gunfire at the Battle of Samar. One was sunk by a German U-Boat. Three were sunk by Japanese kamikaze attacks.

Six of the eight Sun Shipbuilding escort carrier conversions survived World War Two. *Santee* survived strikes by a kamikaze and an aerial torpedo during the 1944 Philippines invasion. *HMS*

Avenger was sunk by a German U-Boat. *HMS Dasher* suffered a catastrophic internal explosion and sank.[16]

Because they were among the first such conversions, numerous problems had to be overcome to make the conversion successful. Lessons learned in both their conversion and operation helped significantly in the design and construction of subsequent escort carriers. In addition, these eight small ships contributed significantly to the training of naval pilots and to the winning of the war at sea against the Axis Powers.

---

[16] Morison, *The Atlantic Battle Won*, p. 39. See Footnote 13 of Morison's book.; "Royal Navy Escort Carriers."

Chapter Two
Sun Shipbuilding

For over 70 years, the Sun Shipbuilding and Drydock Company of Chester, Pennsylvania manufactured ships for the United States government, foreign governments and industrial concerns. Though originally unintended, one of Sun Shipbuilding's most important contributions to the Allied victory was in providing ships for conversion to escort aircraft carriers. Altogether, eight Sun Shipbuilding merchant ships were converted to 'Baby Flattops' for the United States and British Royal Navies.

Sun Shipbuilding was founded in 1916 on the Delaware River in Chester, Pennsylvania, about fifteen miles south of Philadelphia. The shipbuilding company was an offshoot of the Sun Oil Company, who required tanker ships to transport crude oil and petroleum products. Sun's first ship – a 10,600 ton tanker named *Chester Sun* – was launched on 30 October 1917 and delivered to its parent company the following January.[17]

---

[17] Background history on Sun Shipbuilding and Drydock Company was provided by Dave Kavanagh, Founder and President of the Sun Ship Historical Society. See their website www.sunship.org for more information. The data on Chester Sun was taken from a spreadsheet of hull data prepared by the Historical Society: Dave Kavanagh, et. als. "Sun Shipbuilding and Drydock Company Hull Listing." Prepared by the Sun Ship Historical Society. 9 March 2004. [Hereafter cited as "Sun Ship Hull Listing."]

In the years leading up to World War Two, Sun Shipbuilding expanded to become one of the nation's largest shipyards. By the end of the war, it was the largest shipyard in the country with over 35,000 workers and twenty-eight shipways. Sun Shipbuilding constructed 40% of the nation's T2 tankers or some 281 vessels.[18]

Throughout its history, over 600 ships were constructed by Sun Shipbuilding. Primarily these ships were civilian merchant vessels such as cargo ships, tankers and passenger liners. In 1973, Sun Shipbuilding constructed the *Glomar Explorer*, a super-secret deep-sea salvage vessel that was used by the CIA to attempt a recovery of a sunken Soviet missile submarine.[19]

After World War Two, the demand for new ship construction receded and Sun Shipbuilding reduced its operations. No longer needed sections of the massive facility were sub-divided and sold off. The company was bought by Pennsylvania Shipbuilding in 1982 and closed in 1989. Today Sun Ship's yards are now occupied by industrial facilities, a commercial cargo terminal and the Harrah's Chester racetrack and casino.[20]

---

[18] Ibid.

[19] Ibid.

[20] Ibid.

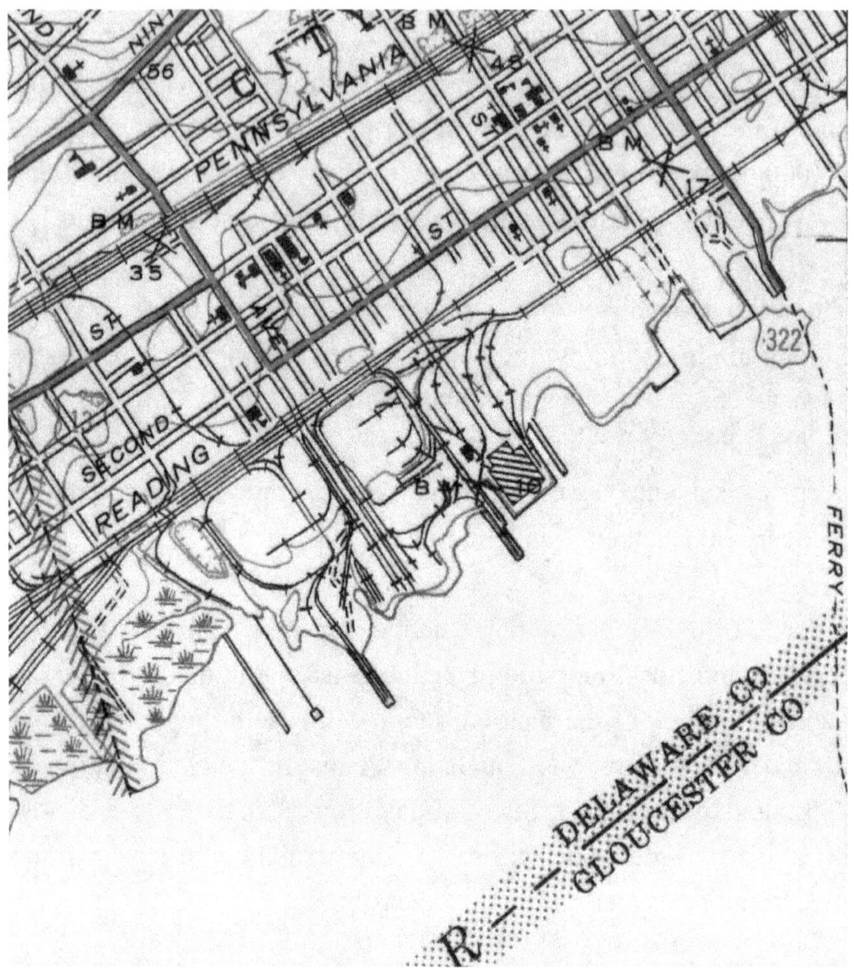

Sun Shipbuilding Site as it appeared on the 1941 U.S. Geological Survey Map "Marcus Hook, PA. - DEL. - N. J." The present day Commodore Barry Bridge is located where the US 322 icon appears on this map.

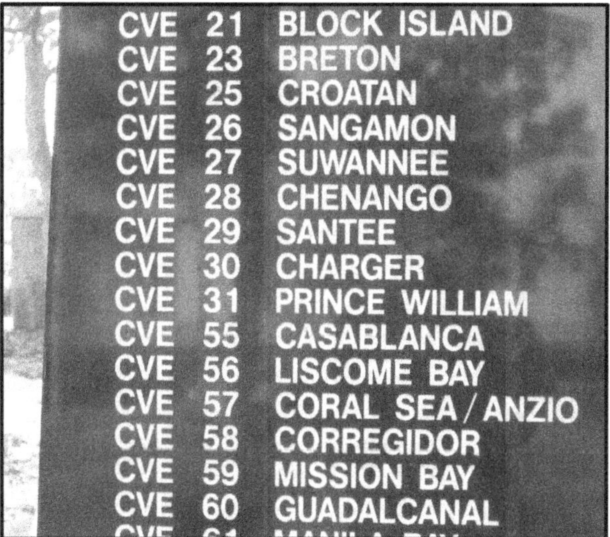

The Aircraft Carrier Memorial in San Diego, California.
(Author's Photos)

Chapter Three
USS Charger (CVE-30)

She never engaged in any battles. Her aircraft never sank or even damaged any enemy ships. Except for two brief forays, she never ventured far from the confines of the Chesapeake Bay. Yet, the escort carrier *USS Charger* (CVE-30) contributed significantly to the defeat of the Axis Powers. US Navy and British Royal Navy pilots that trained upon her flight deck went on to defeat the Imperial Japanese Navy in the Pacific and wrest control of the Atlantic Ocean from the German U-Boats.

Rio de la Plata Becomes *USS Charger*

USS Charger (CVE-30) began her life at Sun Shipbuilding and Dry Dock Company on the banks of the Delaware River as the passenger ship *Rio de la Plata*. She was one of four passenger liners ordered by the Moore-McCormick Line from Sun Shipbuilding. Each of the four ships was named for a South American river. *Rio de la Plata* was launched on 1 March 1941 and was sponsored by Mrs. Courtney Louise Letts Espil, wife of Felipe de Espil, Argentine Ambassador to the United States. *Rio de la Plata* and her sister ships were intended to transport passengers and cargo between New York and the east coast of South America.[21]

Due to the need for aircraft support of trans-Atlantic convoys from German U-Boats, *Rio de la Plata* and her three sisters were purchased by the United States Government in the fall of 1941 for conversion to escort aircraft carriers. Under the Lend-Lease program, all four were transferred to the Royal Navy for their use. *Rio de la Plata* was commissioned as the *HMS Charger* (BAVG-4) with Captain George Abel-Smith, RN, as her first commander. Her tenure with the Royal Navy was brief, however. On 4 October 1941, *Charger* was transferred to the United States Navy. She was re-classified AVG-30.[22]

Today's aircraft carriers are massive. The *Nimitz*-class nuclear-powered carriers are over 1,100 feet long and displace 97,000 tons. The *Nimitz*-class carriers are significantly larger than the Navy's carriers in World War Two. *USS Ranger* (CV-4) was 769 feet long and displaced 14,500 tons. *USS Yorktown* (CV-5) was somewhat larger at 809 feet long and 19,800 tons displacement. The *Essex*-class carriers, which shouldered the brunt of Navy carrier operations, were 872 feet long and displaced 27,100 tons. But even

---

[21] "Post World War II Immigrant Ships: Fairsea." Museum Victoria Fact Sheet (2007). Found online at http://museumvictoria.com.au/ DiscoveryCentre/Infosheets/Fairsea/ ; DANFS. See entry for *USS Charger*.

[22] DANFS. See entry for *USS Charger*.; Scot MacDonald, *Evolution of Aircraft Carriers*. Washington DC GPO: Office of the Chief of Naval Operations, 1962, pp. 49-53.

by World War Two standards, *USS Charger* was small in comparison. Her length was just 492 feet and she displaced only 8,000 tons. *Charger*'s hangar was 190 feet by 47 feet could only hold fifteen aircraft. At best, she could make 16 knots.[23]

After her transfer to the U.S. Navy, *Charger* began the process of conversion to an escort aircraft carrier. She was towed to the Newport News Shipbuilding and Dry Dock Company in Newport News, Virginia, where the conversion work would be performed. The name *Charger* was retained but her designation was changed to AVG-30. On 2 March 1942, *Charger* was towed from Newport News across Hampton Roads to the Norfolk Navy Yard where the Captain of the Yard accepted her. She was tied port side to the dock at Berths 7 and 8.[24]

The following day, 3 March 1942, was a major milestone in the life of *Charger*, ex-*Rio de La Plata*. In early afternoon her new crew was assembled at her berth in the Norfolk Navy Yard. At 1458, Rear Admiral Felix X. Gygax, USN, read OPNAV order 38c BFM serial 38238 (dated 9 February 1942) to the crew, and officially placed *Charger* in commission as a United States naval vessel. Colors were sounded, and the United States Ensign, Union Jack and Commission Pennant were hoisted.[25]

---

[23] See DANFS entries for *Ranger, Yorktown, Essex and Charger*. Data on *Nimitz* provided by www.navy.mil and Robert Hutchinson *Jane's Warship Recognition Guide*. London: HarperCollins, 2002. pp. 42-43.; Captain John Moore, RN, *Jane's American Fighting Ships of the 20th Century,* p.96.

[24] U.S. Navy. *USS Charger*. CVE-30. War Diary. Found in Record Group 38. National Archives and Records Administration. Archives II. College Park, Maryland. (Hereafter cited as "War Diary.")

[25] See War Dairy entry for 3 March 1942.

Then Captain Thomas Lamison Sprague, USN, read BUNAV order Nav-34-AS, 17056-106, Number 19099 (29 January 1942) naming him as commanding officer of *USS Charger* (CVE-30). Thereupon Captain Sprague officially accepted command of the carrier to be. His orders were to complete fitting out of the new ship and then report for duty with the Atlantic Fleet's Carrier Division Three.[26]

In CAPT Sprague, the crew of *USS Charger* was receiving a well-experienced and highly proficient naval aviator and officer. Sprague was born in Ohio in 1894. He graduated from the U.S. Naval Academy in 1917 and was assigned to the cruiser *USS Cleveland*. In April 1918, he was transferred to the new destroyer *USS Montgomery* and was involved with her fitting out. In 1920, he became commander of *Montgomery*. After several years of service in the surface fleet, Sprague decided to join the Navy's fledgeling aviation program. He completed flight training at Naval Air Station Pensacola. Subsequent assignments included commanding Scout Squadrons 6 and 10, staff duty with Commander, Cruisers U.S. Fleet, and serving as superintendent of the engine lab at the Naval Aircraft Factory in Philadelphia, Pennsylvania. In the 1930s, Sprague served as Air Officer aboard the aircraft carrier *USS Saratoga* (CV-3) and Navigator aboard *USS Langley* (CV-1). From 1937 to 1940, he was Superintendent of aviation training at NAS Pensacola. He next served as Executive Officer of *USS Ranger* (CV-4) from 1940 until mid-1941.[27]

---

[26] See War Dairy entry for 3 March 1942.

[27] Samuel Eliot Morison. *History of United States Naval Operations in World War II. Volume XII - Leyte June 1944 - January 1945.* (Boston: Little, Brown & Co., 1958.) See Footnote 16 on page 125.

LCDR Thomas A. Ahroon was assigned to assist with the conversion of *Rio de la Plata* into the escort carrier *Charger* in February 1942 and became a plank owner when she was commissioned the following month.   Thomas Andrew Ahroon was born in Baltimore, Maryland on 3 May 1907 to Dr. Carl R. and Jennie nee Alstrom Ahroon.   He attended Baltimore Polytechnic Institute before receiving an appointment to the U.S. Naval Academy in July 1924.   He graduated with the Class of 1928 and was commissioned as an Ensign.   He served aboard the battleship *USS Arkansas* then reported to NAS Pensacola in March 1930 for flight training.   On 12 December 1930, he was designated a Naval Aviator.   His first aviation assignment was with the aviation detachment aboard the battleship *USS Pennsylvania.*   He served as a Flight Test Pilot at NAS Anacostia, Maryland from July 1934 to June 1937.   His next assignment was aboard the aircraft carrier *USS Yorktown* (CV-5) with Fighting Squadron Five (VF-5).   In August 1940, Ahroon was assigned to NAS Norfolk where he served as Assistant Operations Officer, Communications Officer and Photographic Officer. [28]

Sun Shipbuilding had completed *Charger*'s hull and machinery. Newport News Shipbuilding had added a flight deck. But there was still much work that needed to be completed to make *Charger* ready for operations. CAPT Sprague was ordered to complete extensive alterations to the ship. These alterations included:

1. An island structure was to be installed on the starboard side of the flight deck for the control of air operations

---

[28] U.S. Navy. Office of Information. Biographies Branch. "Rear Admiral Thomas A. Ahroon – United States Navy." 31 March 1960.

2. A mast structure with radar and other equipment necessary for the control of the ship, its air operations and its air defense was to be installed on the island structure.

3. The crew's living and messing spaces were to be re-arranged and bunks installed.

4. The ship's two forward 4-inch surface guns were to be replaced by two 3-inch anti-aircraft guns. Similarly, a 5- inch / 51 gun was to replace the ship's aft 4-inch surface gun.

5. In order to improve stability, topside weight was to be reduced and ballast added below.

6. Watertight integrity was to be improved by eliminating doors and openings in the bulkheads athwartships.

Charger spent the next five weeks completing the necessary alterations. The extensive modifications significantly changed the former merchant ship. The new escort carrier displaced 8,000 tons. At the waterline, her length was 492 feet. She had a beam of 69 feet 6 inches; with her flight deck she was 111 feet 2 inches wide. She had a draft of 26 feet 3 inches. She was powered by an engine that propelled her at a maximum speed of 17 knots on a single shaft. 856 officers and enlisted men manned her.[29]

On 12 April 1942, Captain Sprague sent a message to the Commander in Chief of the U.S. Fleet reporting that *Charger* was

---

[29] DANFS. See entry for *USS Charger.;* Captain John Moore, RN, *Jane's American Fighting Ships of the 20th Century,* p.96.

ready for duty. Soon after, she cast her lines and headed into the Chesapeake Bay on a shakedown cruise.[30]

Charger began flight operations on 27 April 1942 within the Chesapeake Bay. LT C. W. Stewart was the first pilot to land aboard the new escort carrier and perform a take-off. LT Stewart's aircraft was a SOC3A Seagull. Manufactured by the Curtis-Wright Corporation, the SOC was a   single-engine biplane observation plane that could be configured as either a float plane for landing and take-offs on water or with wheels for use on runways and carriers. The SOC3A had fixed wheeled landing gear. LT Stewart was followed by ENS H. A. Kelly of VGS-30 who made the first landing aboard *Charger* by a trainee pilot while at the controls of a Grumman F4F Wildcat fighter. His squadron, Auxiliary Scouting Squadron (VGS-30) Thirty, was the first to train aboard the escort carrier. The VGS designation was assigned to Navy squadrons that were to serve aboard escort carriers. That day, five F4F-4 Wildcats performed ten carrier landings and two SOC3As performed five carrier landings.[31]

Due to insufficient wind, no landings could be performed on 28 April. Instead, five VGS-30 Wildcats conducted flight operations to test *Charger*'s radar. LT Richard Upson performed *Charger*'s first catapult launch in a SOC3A Seagull. Insufficient wind

---

[30] U.S. Navy. *USS Charger.* CVE-30 History of *USS Charger* (CVE-30). 24 May 1945. RG38. NARA. Archives II. See page 2. [Hereafter cited as *Charger* History.];

[31] U.S. Navy. *USS Charger.* CVE-30 History of *USS Charger* (CVE-30). 24 May 1945. RG38. NARA. Archives II. See page 2. [Hereafter cited as *Charger* History.]; U.S. Navy. Auxiliary Scouting Squadron Thirty (VGS-30). War Diary. April 1942. RG38, NARA, Archives II.;

cancelled landings on 29 April as well. Three VGS-30 Wildcats rendezvoused with *Charger* for a radar tracking exercise.[32]

Winds were sufficient for carrier landings on 1 May. Six Wildcats did eight carrier landings and two SOC3A did two carrier landings. Two days later, five Wildcats F4F4s did nine carrier landings, two SOC3As did two carrier landings. ENS W. Sweetman in a F4F-4 Wildcat crashed while attempting to land. Most likely his was probably the first crash aboard *Charger*.[33]

On her shakedown cruise, problems emerged with her main engine similar to those experienced by her sister ship *Avenger*. Engine difficulties limited the ship's top speed to fourteen knots. On 2 May 1942, Captain Sprague sent a message requesting that *Charger* be brought into the Norfolk Navy Yard to correct the engine problems. Approved for repairs, *Charger* entered the Navy Yard the following week and work commenced on correcting her engine problems.[34]

When the repair work was completed, *Charger* reported to the Commander, Air Force, Atlantic Fleet (Task Force 28) for duty and was assigned to Fleet Air Command, Norfolk (Task Group 28.1). *Charger* did not have any aircraft permanently assigned to her except for two or three amphibious planes. She had a Shore Based Detachment which worked out of Hangar LP-3 at East Field, Naval

---

[32] U.S. Navy. Auxiliary Scouting Squadron Thirty (VGS-30). War Diary. April 1942. RG38, NARA, Archives II.

[33] U.S. Navy. Auxiliary Scouting Squadron Thirty (VGS-30). War Diary. May 1942. RG38, NARA, Archives II.

[34] *Charger* War Diary. See entries for April and May 1942.

Air Station Norfolk. She also worked in conjunction with Carrier Air Support Unit 21 (CASU-21).[35]

For the rest of the summer, she operated in the Chesapeake Bay and its immediate vicinity. On 20 August 1942, the ship was re-classified ACV-30.[36]

Another of the first squadrons to operate from the new escort carrier was Navy Escort Fighting Squadron Twenty-Nine (VGF-29). Formed by Lieutenant Commander Tom Blackburn, VGF-29 consisted of twelve F4F Wildcat fighters. At the time, the Wildcats were the U.S. Navy's top fighter. Escort Fighting Squadron Twenty-Nine (VGF-29) was commissioned on 18 July 1942 at 0830 under the command of LCDR J. T. Blackburn, USN. The squadron was equipped with F4F Wildcats and trained to operate off the Navy's new escort carriers. As such, VGF-29 conducted much training with *USS Charger* (AVG-30). While performing carrier qualifications, ENS F. G. Barnes was killed in a plane crash on 8 August 1942.[37]

---

[35] U.S. Navy. *USS Charger.* CVE-30 History of *USS Charger* (CVE-30). 24 May 1945. RG38. NARA. Archives II. [Hereafter cited as *Charger* History.]

[36] *Charger* War Diary. See entries for May through August 1942.

[37] Tom Blackburn and Eric Hammel. *The Jolly Rogers: The Story of Tom Blackburn and Navy Fighting Squadron VF-17.* St. Paul, MN: Zenith P, 1998. p. 19.; U.S. Navy. Escort Fighting Squadron Twenty-Nine. VGF-29. War Diary. 18 July 1942 to 31 October 1942. RG38, NARA, Archives II.

Chapter Four
Operation Torch

In the summer of 1942, plans were well underway to begin offensive operations against Nazi Germany and Fascist Italy. Much to the chagrin of senior American military and naval leaders, this first Allied offensive operation would not be an amphibious assault to liberate the Continent of Europe but an assault against Axis forces in North Africa. Codenamed Operation Torch, the Allied invasion of North Africa would take place at three separate locations along the coast. Initially the landing would take place against the Vichy French, though it was expected that the Germans would respond quickly and vigorously. The Allies landing in North Africa would coordinate with British Lieutenant General Sir Bernard Montgomery's Eighth Army then driving west across North Africa from Egypt.

Operation Torch was a highly complicated affair. Most of the American forces would be directly traveling from the United States. Operation Torch would include some of America's most promising military and naval leaders. The Western Task Force's

Army component was commanded by Major General George S. Patton Jr. Naval forces were commanded by Rear Admiral Kent Hewitt. Landing clandestinely before the invasion to secure French cooperation for the invasion was Major General Mark Clark. Overall command of the invasion was Major General Dwight D. Eisenhower.

The United States Navy would be providing assault ships, aircraft carriers and battleships and cruisers for naval gunfire support. The U.S. aircraft carriers included the escort carrier *USS Charger* (AVG-30).

While *Charger* was fitting out and starting to train pilots for carrier warfare, major developments were occurring with the Second World War. In early May 1942, a task force built around *USS Lexington* (CV-2) and *USS Yorktown* (CV-5) fought naval history's first naval battle in which the combatants never saw each other. The two American carriers took on two Japanese fleet carriers and one light carrier. *Lexington* was sunk and *Yorktown* was seriously damaged. The Japanese lost the light carrier *Shoho* but more importantly, were forced to abandon their plan to invade Port Moresby and thus threaten the sea lanes between Australia and the United States. Barely a month later, the U.S. and Imperial Japanese Navy fought the epic Battle of Midway in the Central Pacific. Four Japanese aircraft carriers and *USS Yorktown* were sunk in a huge victory for the U.S. In August 1942, U.S. Marines invaded Guadalcanal in the Solomon Islands and a long, brutal series ground, air and naval battles ensued for control of these vital islands. In the Atlantic Theater, German U-Boats were devastating Allied ships right off the American coast.

For the moment, U.S. ground forces had not entered the war in the European Theater. That was all about to change. Plans were underway for Operation Torch. Instead of attacking Adolf Hitler's Festung Europa directly, British Prime Minister Winston Churchill convinced the American high command to attack North Africa first and clear it of Axis Forces. The plan was to land some 73,500 British and American forces on three areas of French Morocco and Algeria on the North African coast. As these areas were occupied by Vichy France, the Allies would be confronting not German forces but Vichy French allied with the Germans. Through skillful diplomacy, the Allies hoped to persuade the French not to oppose the landings. U.S. Army General Dwight D. Eisenhower was placed in command of the combined British – American force.[38]

As part of Torch, Task Force 34 would land 37,000 U.S. troops under the command of Major General George S. Patton, Jr. at three locations on the coast of Morocco. To support Patton's amphibious assault, Rear Admiral Kent Hewitt's force included the battleships *USS New York* (BB-34), *USS Texas* (BB-35) and *USS Massachusetts* (BB-59), the aircraft carrier *USS Ranger* (CV-4), four escort carriers, three heavy cruisers, four light cruisers and thirty-eight destroyers. Because Morocco was controlled by the French Vichy government allied with Germany, the Americans

---

[38] *Algeria-French Morocco.* In the series *The U.S. Army Campaigns of World War II.* CMH Publication 72-11. (Washington DC: U.S. Army Center of Military History, 1995).; Samuel Eliot Morison, *Operations in North African Waters: October 1942 to June 1943.* Volume II In the series *History of United States Naval Operations in World War II.* (Boston: Brown, Little & Co., 1947).

would be facing the French Army and Navy instead of the Germans.[39]

To support the Morocco landings, the U.S. Atlantic Fleet was providing the aircraft carrier *USS Ranger* (CV-4), and four escort carriers. The escort carriers were *USS Santee* (ACV-29), *USS Sangamon* (ACV-26), *USS Chenango* (ACV-28) and *USS Charger* (AVG-30). The five carriers and their escorts were organized into Task Force 22. The task force was sub-divided into four task groups:

Task Group 22.1 Aircraft Carriers - *Ranger, Charger*
       Destroyers - Destroyer Division 20
        (DESDIV 20) *Fitch* (DD-462),
        Forrest (DD-461), *Corry* (DD-463),
        Hobson (DD-464) plus *Ellyson* (DD-454)

Task Group 22.2 Aircraft Carrier – *Sangamon*
       Destroyers - *Hambleton* (DD-455),
         Macombs (DD-458)

Task Group 22.3 Aircraft Carrier - *Santee*
       Destroyers – *Rodman* (DD-456),
        Emmons (DD-457)

Task Group 22.4 Aircraft Carrier – *Chenango*

Unassigned Cruisers - *Augusta* (CA-31),
        Cleveland (CL-55)

---

[39] Ibid.

Aircraft Carrier - *Suwannee*[40]

Air support would be absolutely critical to the success of not only the initial amphibious landings but subsequent operations ashore as well. Until airfields could be established ashore, the Navy would have to provide the air support from its aircraft carriers. But 1942 had been a tough one for the Navy's fleet aircraft carriers. *Lexington* had been sunk at the Coral Sea in May. *Yorktown* went down the following month at Midway. *Wasp* was lost to a Japanese submarine in September. *Hornet* was sunk in October at the Battle of Santa Cruz. That left just *Enterprise, Saratoga,* and *Ranger.* Since *Enterprise* and *Saratoga* were desperately needed in the Pacific, the Navy was forced to rely upon its hastily converted escort carriers to provide naval air support for Operation Torch.

On 1 October, *Charger* was ordered to join the Atlantic Fleet's Task Force 22, Task Group 22.1. On 3 October 1942, Task Group 22.1 sortied from Naval Operating Base Norfolk. Their destination was Naval Operating Base Bermuda. There, Task Force 22 would assemble, complete final preparation and training and then sortie to join up with the Western Naval Task Force (TF34) for Operation Torch. The weather was rather pleasant on the day that TG 22.1 departed from NOB Norfolk. The seas were moderate with a 16-knot wind from the north-east.[41]

---

[40] U.S. Navy. Atlantic Fleet. Carriers, Atlantic Fleet. War Diary for Period 1 October 1942 to 23 October 1942. 23 October 1942. RG38, NARA, Archives II.

[41] U.S. Navy. Atlantic Fleet. Carriers, Atlantic Fleet. War Diary for Period 1 October 1942 to 23 October 1942. 23 October 1942. RG38, NARA, Archives II.; U.S. Navy. *USS Charger.* (CVE-30). War Diary for the Month of October 1942. RG38, NARA, Archives II.

Though Bermuda was a British possession, the U.S. Navy had been using the island group as a result of the September 1940 Destroyers for Bases deal worked out between Prime Minister Churchill and President Roosevelt. In return for fifty old U.S. Navy destroyers, the British granted basing rights to Bermuda and a number of its other possessions in the Western Hemisphere. It was a rather crafty deal because the arrangement essentially made the United States responsible for the defense of these possessions and freed up British forces to be used elsewhere.

Though Escort Fighting Squadron Twenty-Nine had trained aboard *USS Charger* over the summer, the squadron was not destined to go to war aboard her. When *Charger* sailed for Bermuda on 3 October, VGF-29 was not aboard her. VGF-29 embarked on *USS Santee* (ACV-29) on 8 October 1942.[42]

The voyage to NOB Bermuda was relatively uneventful, despite the fact that the Battle of the Atlantic was raging. At 0715 on 4 October, *Ranger* launched five SBD Dauntless dive-bombers for anti-submarine patrols around the task group. Three hours later, she launched three more Dauntlesses for anti-submarine patrols. At 0650 the next day, *Ranger* and three destroyers separated from *Charger, Hobson* and *Fitch* to conduct flight operations. The weather was clear with winds blowing 12 to 15 knots from the north-east. At 1615, *Charger* began conducting her own flight operations. She launched eleven Wildcat fighters and landed them one hour later. The task group re-assembled at 1935 and the

---

[42] U.S. Navy. Escort Fighting Squadron Twenty-Nine. VGF-29. War Diary. 18 July 1942 to 31 October 1942. RG38, NARA, Archives II.

destroyers formed an anti-submarine screen around the two carriers.[43]

On 6 October 1942, Task Group 22.1 was nearing Naval Operating Base Bermuda. At 0726, *Ranger* and *Charger* again separated for air operations. At 0738 *Charger* launched eleven Wildcats to land at Bermuda's Kindley Field. At 0920 F4F Wildcat and SBD Dauntless aircraft from *Ranger* and *Charger* began arriving at Kindley Field. The task group ships all actually steamed to the north of Bermuda and then circled back to enter Bermuda from the east. At 1000, *Ranger, Charger* and their escorting destroyers entered the main channel. At 1115, the carriers anchored in Grassy Bay while the destroyers anchored in Port Royal Bay.[44]

Beginning on 7 October 1942, Task Group 22.1 conducted training operations in the waters around Bermuda. On 7 October, *Ranger,* and the destroyers *Fitch, Forrest* and *Corry* steamed out of their anchorages and conducted air operations and AA practice. *Ranger* returned to NOB Bermuda at 0915 the following morning.[45]

---

[43] U.S. Navy. Atlantic Fleet. Carriers, Atlantic Fleet. War Diary for Period 1 October 1942 to 23 October 1942. 23 October 1942. RG38, NARA, Archives II.

[44] U.S. Navy. Atlantic Fleet. Carriers, Atlantic Fleet. War Diary for Period 1 October 1942 to 23 October 1942. 23 October 1942. RG38, NARA, Archives II.; U.S. Navy. Naval Operating Base Bermuda. War Diary for October 1942. RG38, NARA, Archives II.; There is a slight discrepancy between the times listed in both War Diaries for the arrival of Task Group 22.1.; U.S. Navy. *USS Charger.* (CVE-30). War Diary for the Month of October 1942. RG38, NARA, Archives II.

[45] U.S. Navy. Naval Operating Base Bermuda. War Diary for October 1942. RG38, NARA, Archives II.

At 0810 on the morning of 8 October 1942, *Charger got* underway for exercises which also included *Ellyson, Fitch, Corry,* and *Forrest* and two older submarines *USS R-1* and *USS R-7.* At 0910, Navy patrol plane 52-P-6 took off to cover the *Charger* exercise. Intelligence reports indicated that two German U-Boats were operating in region. Short range battle practice was conducted. The weather was excellent that day. There were scattered clouds, and visibility and ceiling unlimited. The winds were blowing 8 to 12 knots out of the north-east and the temperature ranged from 73 to 83 degrees during the day. At 1740, *Charger* returned from her exercises.[46]

9 October was another day of training exercises. At 0915 *Corry, R1* and *R7* departed for an exercise with *Corry.* At 0950 Navy patrol plane 52-P-6 took off to cover *Charger*'s exercise. At 1131 *Charger* and the destroyers *Ellyson, Forrest,* and *Fitch* got underway. Out at sea, the ships performed anti-aircraft gunnery practice. The weather was scattered clouds, isolated showers and visility from 8 to 10 miles. There were gentle to moderate winds out of the southeast. Ceiling was unlimited and the temperature ranged between 72 and 80 degrees. At 1730 *Charger,* her escorts, *Corry, R1* and *R7* all returned to their Bermuda anchorages.[47]

---

[46] U.S. Navy. Atlantic Fleet. Carriers, Atlantic Fleet. War Diary for Period 1 October 1942 to 23 October 1942. 23 October 1942. RG38, NARA, Archives II.; U.S. Navy. Naval Operating Base Bermuda. War Diary for October 1942. RG38, NARA, Archives II.; U.S. Navy. *USS Charger.* (CVE-30). War Diary for the Month of October 1942. RG38, NARA, Archives II.

[47] U.S. Navy. Atlantic Fleet. Carriers, Atlantic Fleet. War Diary for Period 1 October 1942 to 23 October 1942. 23 October 1942. RG38, NARA, Archives II.; U.S. Navy. Naval Operating Base Bermuda. War Diary for October 1942. RG38, NARA, Archives II.; U.S. Navy. *USS Charger.* (CVE-30). War Diary for the Month of October 1942. RG38, NARA, Archives II.

On 10 October, *Charger* suffered an aviation mishap. Aircraft GF9 was being catapulted when a cable broke. With insufficient speed to get airborne, the aircraft quickly plummeted into the water. Though the aircraft was lost, the pilot was recovered.[48]

Meanwhile, some significant changes were underway for Task Force 22 and specifically for *USS Charger*. Task Group 22.2 was en route for NOB Bermuda with the escort carrier *USS Sangamon* and destroyers *USS Hambleton* and *USS Macombs*. Steaming independently were the light cruiser *USS Cleveland* and the destroyer *USS Hobson*. Task Force 22 commanding officer RADM Earnest D. McWhorter was aboard *Cleveland*. *Cleveland* and *Hobson* arrived early on the afternoon of 12 October 1942. RADM McWhorter transferred his flag to *Ranger* at 1410. Most importantly for *Charger,* she was being sent back to NOB Norfolk.[49]

On 12 October 1942, *Charger* made ready to depart NOB Bermuda bound for NOB Norfolk. At 1115, *Ellyson, Fitch, Forrest* and *Corry* sortied from Port Royal Bay and conducted an anti-submarine sweep of the vicinity. The decision having been made to send *Charger* back to Norfolk, the escort carrier got underway at 1254. At 1346, *Charger* rendezvoused with the four destroyers who formed an anti-submarine screen around her. They headed

---

[48] U.S. Navy. *USS Charger.* (CVE-30). War Diary for the Month of October 1942. RG38, NARA, Archives II.

[49] U.S. Navy. Atlantic Fleet. Carriers, Atlantic Fleet. War Diary for Period 1 October 1942 to 23 October 1942. 23 October 1942. RG38, NARA, Archives II.; U.S. Navy. Naval Operating Base Bermuda. War Diary for October 1942. RG38, NARA, Archives II.

west for Norfolk zig-zagging at sixteen knots. *Ellyson* set Condition II watch with two five-inch guns, her torpedo tubes, depth charges, intel center, plotting rooms and two 20mm guns manned. At 1810 Navy patrol plane 52-P-1 took off for night coverage over *Charger* and her escorts. There were a few local showers that day. Ceiling was generally unlimited with visibility 8 to 10 miles, light westerly winds, and temperatures between 74 and 82 degrees.[50]

Charger's voyage back to Norfolk was uneventful. On 14 October, she and her escorts pulled into NOB Norfolk. The following day, *Charger* reported for duty to Chief of Air Operational Training. Apparently, *Charger* would not be participating in Operation Torch.[51]

Three days after pulling into NOB Norfolk, *Corry* and *Fitch* got underway headed for NOB Bermuda again. This time, they would

---

[50] U.S. Navy. Atlantic Fleet. Carriers, Atlantic Fleet. War Diary for Period 1 October 1942 to 23 October 1942. 23 October 1942. RG38, NARA, Archives II.; U.S. Navy. Atlantic Fleet. *USS Ellyson* (DD-454). War Diary. October 1942. RG38, NARA, Archives II.; U.S. Navy. Naval Operating Base Bermuda. War Diary for October 1942. RG38, NARA, Archives II. Again, there are slight time discrepancies between the NOB Bermuda War Diary and the Carriers, Atlantic Fleet War Diary.; U.S. Navy. *USS Charger.* (CVE-30). War Diary for the Month of October 1942. RG38, NARA, Archives II.

[51] U.S. Navy. Atlantic Fleet. Carriers, Atlantic Fleet. War Diary for Period 1 October 1942 to 23 October 1942. 23 October 1942. RG38, NARA, Archives II.; U.S. Navy. *USS Charger.* (CVE-30). War Diary for the Month of October 1942. RG38, NARA, Archives II.

be escorting the new escort carrier *USS Suwannee* (ACV-27). *Suwannee* had nine TBF Avengers of VGS-30 embarked aboard.[52]

Suwannee had begun her existence as *Markay*, a Maritime Commission tanker constructed by the Federal Shipbuilding and Drydock Company of Kearney, New Jersey. Her keel was laid on 3 June 1938. She was launched on 4 March 1939 and initially operated by the Keystone Tankship Corporation. On 26 June 1941, the Navy acquired her, renamed her *USS Suwanne* (AO-33) and placed her in commission on 16 July 1941. After six months of operations with the Atlantic Fleet, the Navy decommissioned her on 21 February 1942 at Newport News Shipbuilding and Dry Dock Company in Newport News, Virginia. There she was converted to an escort aircraft carrier. On 24 September 1942, *USS Suwannee* (ACV-27) was placed in commission under the command of CAPT J. J. Clark, USN. After conversion to an aircraft carrier, *Suwannee* had a length of 553 feet, a beam of 75 feet, and a draft of 31 feet 7 inches. She displaced 7,500 tons. Her flight deck was 502 feet long and 84 feet wide. Ship and flight operations were controlled from a small island located well forward on the starboard side.[53]

---

[52] U.S. Navy. Atlantic Fleet. Carriers, Atlantic Fleet. War Diary for Period 1 October 1942 to 23 October 1942. 23 October 1942. RG38, NARA, Archives II.; U.S. Navy. Task Force 22. *USS Suwannee* (ACV-27). War Diary. September 24, 1942 to November 1, 1942. RG38, NARA, Archives II.; DANFS Entry for *USS Suwannee* https://www.history.navy.mil/research/histories/ship-histories/danfs/s/suwannee.html

[53] U.S. Navy. Task Force 22. *USS Suwannee* (ACV-27). War Diary. September 24, 1942 to November 1, 1942. RG38, NARA, Archives II.; DANFS Entry for *USS Suwannee* https://www.history.navy.mil/research/histories/ship-histories/danfs/s/suwannee.html

Operation Torch was less than two months away when *Suwannee* was placed in commission. Her commanding officer CAPT J. J. Clark rushed to get her into service in time for Operation Torch. He got the commissioning date advanced, then cut down the ship's fitting out period by a week and cut her Chesapeake Bay training operations short by two weeks. On 17 October 1942, *Suwannee* was ready for war. So it was decided to send her to Bermuda to join the Navy forces assembling for Operation Torch.[54]

At 1040 on 17 October, *Suwannee* with nine TBF Avengers of VGS-30 embarked set sail from Norfolk accompanied by the destroyers *Corry* and *Fitch*. Two days later, *Suwannee, Corry* and *Fitch* entered Bermuda and dropped anchor in Murray's Anchorage. She was assigned to Task Group 22.1.[55]

The day after arriving, *Suwannee* experienced a serious aviation mishap during flight operations. At 1449, a F4F-4 Wildcat was being prepared for catapult launch. The pilot had not yet gotten into the aircraft. Suddenly and without warning, the Wildcat was unintentionally launched off the flight deck.   The unmanned Wildcat hit the water and quickly sank in 11 fathoms of water at 32

---

[54] U.S. Navy. Task Force 22. *USS Suwannee* (ACV-27). War Diary. September 24, 1942 to November 1, 1942. RG38, NARA, Archives II.; DANFS Entry for *USS Suwannee* https://www.history.navy.mil/research/histories/ship-histories/danfs/s/ suwannee.html ; U.S. Navy. Bureau of Aeronautics. Interview of CAPT J. J. Clark, USN. *USS Suwannee.* In the Bureau of Aeronautics 27 November 1942. RG38, NARA, Archives II.;

[55] U.S. Navy. Task Force 22. *USS Suwannee* (ACV-27). War Diary. September 24, 1942 to November 1, 1942. RG38, NARA, Archives II.; DANFS Entry for *USS Suwannee* https://www.history.navy.mil/research/histories/ship-histories/danfs/s/ suwannee.html

degrees 22 minutes 7 seconds North latitude, 63 degrees 37 minutes 9 seconds W longitude. The human cost, however, was high. Electricians Mate 3rd Class George Martin Pridmore and Aviation Metalsmith 3rd Class Dale Earl Kerr of VGS-27, Seaman 2nd Class James Michael Dente, Seaman 2nd Class Robert Francis Doherty and Seaman 2nd Class Kenneth Arthur Doyle of VGF-27, and Aviation Machinists Mate 3rd Class Alpha Earl Coates of *Suwannee* were all injured.   Dente and Doherty later died of their injuries. Seaman 2nd Class Thomas Bernard Derby and Seaman 2nd Class William Edgar Canham of VGS-27 were knocked over the side and into the water.   Both sailors were lost and their bodies never recovered.[56]

Operation Torch commenced in the pre-dawn hours of 8 November 1942.   Despite some early confusion and stronger than expected French resistance, American and British troops stormed ashore and moved inland. In the succeeding days, all French resistance ended and American and British troops established themselves ashore. The operation was successful though not without its difficulties. Many more months of heavy fighting lay ahead and the final defeat of Axis Forces in North Africa would not happen until 13 May 1943.

Suwanee's shakedown cruise was participating in Operation Torch. Task Force 22 departed Bermuda on 21 October 1942.   While at sea, eleven F4F-4 Wildcats from VGF-27, twelve F4F-4 Wildcats from VGF-28 and six F4F-4 Wildcats from VGS-30 landed aboard

---

[56] U.S. Navy. Task Force 22. *USS Suwannee* (ACV-27). War Diary. September 24, 1942 to November 1, 1942. RG38, NARA, Archives II.; DANFS Entry for *USS Suwannee*
https://www.history.navy.mil/research/histories/ship-histories/danfs/s/suwannee.html

to complete *Suwannee*'s air group.   Task Force 22 arrived off the coast of Morocco on 8 November 1942.   As part of the Center Attack Group, *Suwannee*'s aircraft supported the amphibious assault on Morocco. Her aircraft carried out 255 air sorties. Three were lost in combat and two were lost to operational causes.[57]

Soon after returning from Operation Torch, CAPT J. J. Clark was interviewed by the Bureau of Aeronautics about his role in the invasion.   In the interview, CAPT Clark commented upon his carrier's embarked squadrons.   He stated:

> The squadrons which I had were well trained. They had been trained by the CHARGER. They had been operating since last March; so that they had lots of landings on the CHARGER; none of the pilots that I had were green. It might have been different on some other ships; but I had my own fighter squadron and the pilots were all old timers. My TBF's had been in training and been operating from the CHARGER.[58]

On 19 October 1942, *Suwannee* and her escorts entered Bermuda's harbor.   Seven days earlier, *Charger* and her escorting destroyers had departed Bermuda. With *Suwannee* operational, *Charger* was no longer needed for Operation Torch. This was an interesting turn

---

[57] U.S. Navy. Task Force 22. *USS Suwannee* (ACV-27). War Diary. September 24, 1942 to November 1, 1942. RG38, NARA, Archives II.; DANFS Entry for *USS Suwannee*
https://www.history.navy.mil/research/histories/ship-histories/danfs/s/suwannee.html

[58] U.S. Navy. Bureau of Aeronautics. Interview of CAPT J. J. Clark, USN. *USS Suwannee.* In the Bureau of Aeronautics 27 November 1942. RG38, NARA, Archives II. See page 10.

of events. *Charger* had been operational since April and had conducted hundreds of carrier landings. Her crew was well trained and ready for war. So why was she was replaced by another escort carrier that had been rushed into service only a few weeks prior?

This question was posed to *Suwannee*'s commanding officer CAPT J. J. Clark during the Bureau of Aeronautics interview. *Suwannee* was chosen to replace *Charger* because *Charger* was smaller and slower than *Suwannee*. As CAPT Clark explained,

> The CHARGER was originally in the operation and the SUWANNEE was out; by being able to cut corners here and there, we gained a full three or four weeks on our readiness. We picked up one week on the date of commission, another week on the fitting out, and we did, in ten days, what we were supposed to do in 24 days; so we really got pretty far ahead of the gate. It became evident that we could be ready if they wanted to make the change. Without intending to route them out of their position, we just simply happened to be ready and they took us instead.[59]

There was another reason why *Charger* was replaced by *Suwannee*. According to Motor Machinists Mate 3rd Class Andrew S. Futey who joined the ship in April 1944, *Charger* had had stability issues during its voyage to Bermuda. This had been *Charger*'s first venture out from the confines of the Chesapeake Bay and apparently issues with its seaworthiness had arisen.

---

[59] U.S. Navy. Bureau of Aeronautics. Interview of CAPT J. J. Clark, USN. *USS Suwannee.* In the Bureau of Aeronautics 27 November 1942. RG38, NARA, Archives II. See page 11.

Thus, *Charger* would return to Norfolk and miss out on the North Africa invasion, while *Suwannee* would not only serve with distinction in Operation Torch but also in the Pacific Theater as well.

Chapter Five
After Torch:
Charger from November 1942
to December 1943

Though her crew probably didn't realize it at the time, Operation Torch would be *Charger*'s one and only chance to participate in combat operations.   *Charger* returned to NOB Norfolk and resumed training pilots for other aircraft carriers going to war. For the next twelve months, *Charger* would work tirelessly to ensure that carrier pilots were ready to take the war to the Axis Powers from U.S. Navy and British Royal Navy flight decks.

Upon its return to NOB Norfolk, *Charger* was assigned to Carriers, U.S. Atlantic Fleet Task Force 31.2. TF 31.2 was comprised of vessels not under operational control of the Fleet's other task force commanders. *Charger* returned to her duties training pilots. She conducted flight operations in Chesapeake Bay and ended the month anchored in the operating area. In total, *Charger* had 31 landings in October, including during her brief foray to Bermuda and back.[60]

Flight operations resumed on 1 November. That day *Charger* experienced two aviation mishaps. First, a SB2C-2 Helldiver crashed into the Number 18 20mm gun position while attempting to land. The Helldiver was severely damaged but no personnel were injured. Then, a Royal Navy TBF Avenger struck the ramp of the after edge of the flight deck. The Avenger sustained minor damage but there were no personnel injuries. On 10 November, *Charger* experienced its third mishap of the month when a SNJ3C failed to catch the arresting wires and crashed into the crash barrier. The SNJ was slightly damaged and there were no injuries to pilot or ship's company. Another SNJ-3C had a similar mishap on 20 November with similar results. The next day, however, a TBF Avenger failed to engage the arresting wires, plunged over the side and into the water. The Avenger was lost but the pilot was recovered. A SB2C2 Helldiver failed to engage the arresting wires on 27 November but with better results. The Helldiver hit the crash barrier and suffered only slight damage. The final mishap of the month occurred on 30 November when a SNJ-3 caught the Number Six arresting wire but slid into the starboard catwalk. The SNJ was only slightly damaged and no one was injured. Altogether, there were seven mishaps during the month of November, and one aircraft lost overboard, and 1,107 successful landings. Also during this month. LCDR Thomas A. Ahroon was appointed as the ship's Air Officer.[61]

---

[60] U.S. Navy. *USS Charger.* (CVE-30). War Diary for the Month of October 1942. RG38, NARA, Archives II.

[61] U.S. Navy. USS Charger. (CVE-30). War Diary for the Month of November 1942. RG38, NARA, Archives II.

Flight operations were conducted on eleven days in December 1942. Heavy snow and fog cancelled flight operations on five days that month. There were five serious aviation mishaps that month. On 10 December 1942, ENS A. H. Sparrow landed a SB2U-2 Vindicator aboard but slipped into the port catwalk. The damaged aircraft was stowed below on the Hangar Deck. Sub-Lieutenant C. S. Hyde of the Royal Navy had a barrier crash that resulted in heavy damage to his aircraft and lacerations to his face and scalp on 17 December. There were two mishaps on 19 December. ENS S. F. Garton ran off the flight deck and into the port catwalk with his SB2U-2 Vindicator. Then, ENS William Reiter repeated the feat in a FM1 Wildcat. The last mishap of the month was the most serious. On 28 December, ENS C. L. Wilson crashed into the water on landing approach. His TBF Avenger sank immediately. He was recovered by the plane guard ship and treated for moderate exposure.[62]

Midway through the month, *Charger* took a break from its flight operations to conduct a very important ceremony. After recording its 4,000th landing aboard ship, *Charger* left the operating area and returned to NOB Norfolk. She tied up to Pier #5. In a ceremony held aboard ship, CAPT Grover B. H. Hall relieved CAPT Sprague of command of *Charger.* After the Change of Command ceremony, *Charger* got underway and returned to the operating area for flight operations.[63]

---

[62] U.S. Navy. *USS Charger.* CVE-30. Deck Log. December 1942. RG38, NARA, Archives II.

[63] U.S. Navy. *USS Charger.* CVE-30. Deck Log. December 1942. RG38, NARA, Archives II.

CAPT Sprague then reported to Commander, Carrier Replacement Squadrons – Atlantic Fleet for duty involving flying as Aide and Chief of Staff. In August of 1943, Sprague commissioned his second aircraft carrier – the *Essex*-class carrier *USS Intrepid* (CV-11). Under his command, *Intrepid* conducted air strikes throughout the Pacific during the first half of 1944. In June 1944, he was promoted to Rear Admiral and placed in command of Carrier Division 22 and Task Group 77.4. On 25 October 1944, his TG77.4 took on a powerful force of Japanese surface warships including the super battleship *Yamato*. Despite the overwhelming odds, his plucky little escort carriers and destroyers and destroyer-escorts managed to survive the ordeal at a loss of two carriers and several destroyers. For his heroism, Sprague was awarded the Navy Cross. He next commanded Carrier Division 3 during the Okinawa invasion. Then he commanded Task Force 38.1 for the final air strikes against the Japanese Home Islands.[64]

Charger remained in the Chesapeake Bay for the duration of the war. Her mission was to qualify U.S. Navy and Royal Navy pilots in carrier operations. Typically, *Charger* would steam from either the Norfolk Navy Yard or an anchorage in nearby Hampton Roads and proceed to an operating area in the lower Chesapeake Bay. There she would conduct flight operations during the day and oftentimes at night as well. When flight operations were completed for the day, she would anchor in the operating area overnight and resume operations the next day. This cycle would be repeated for several days or weeks at a time.

---

[64] See Morison, *Leyte June 1944 - January 1945* for more details about Rear Admiral Sprague's role in the Battle off Samar.; U.S. Navy. *USS Charger. CVE-30* History of *USS Charger* (CVE-30). 24 May 1945. RG38. NARA. Archives II. [Hereafter cited as *Charger* History.]

Landing aboard the small flight deck of this escort carrier was no easy feat. With a flight deck less than five hundred feet long, flight operations aboard *USS Charger* were often a dangerous affair. If a pilot failed to catch one of the arresting cables strung across the aft of the flight deck, he could apply power and circle around for another attempt. Oftentimes, a cable barrier was strung across the flight deck to catch planes that missed the arresting wires. Motor Machinist Mate 3rd Class Andrew Futey recalled witnessing several planes crash on deck or over the side of the flight deck.[65]

The New Year: 1943

The deck logs do not contain a running tally of landings aboard *USS Charger*, nor do they record which squadrons were conducting flight operations in conjunction with her. The deck logs do provide a much more detailed account of *Charger*'s movements and oftentimes provide the name of pilots involved in aviation mishaps.

USS Charger was underway and conducting flight operations on the very first day of 1943. At 1325, a TBF-1 Avenger piloted by ENS Donald K. Sahlolom successfully caught one of the arresting wires but the wire parted and his Avenger careened into the barrier. He was uninjured and his plane was only slightly damaged but two *Charger* sailors suffered lacerations of the face from being struck by the parted wire.   Fireman 2nd Class Walter H. Edwards and Motor Machinists Mate 2nd Class Charles V. Rankin were treated in the ship's sick bay.[66]

---

[65] On several occasions, my grandfather described watching the pilots training (and not always landing) aboard *Charger* to me.

[66] U.S. Navy. *USS Charger.* CVE-30. Deck Log. January 1943. RG38, NARA, Archives II. See entry for 1 January 1943.

Over the next five days, there were four mishaps aboard the training carrier. At 1604 on 2 January, ENS F. F. Norris's SB2U2 Helldiver caught the Number Four wire but slid sideways into the port walkway. He was uninjured and his aircraft suffered only slight damage. At 1228 on 3 January, ENS C. P. Hardesty missed the arresting wires, jumped the barrier, went over the port side of the carrier and crashed into the water. His SNJ trainer aircraft was lost but he was rescued by the plane guard ship. Two days later, two F4F Wildcats piloted by LT(jg) A. E. Linder and ENS Spero Constantine crashed during the landing attempts. Neither pilot was injured and their respective Wildcats suffered minor damage.[67]

The most serious mishap aboard *Charger* occurred on 12 January. At 0956, ENS Gordon G. Behrens was at the controls of a FM2 Wildcat preparing for take-off. When given the command, ENS Behrens went to full throttle and roared down *Charger*'s short flight deck. Something happened that caused Behrens's Wildcat to crash into the water a mere thirty feet in front of the escort carrier. On the bridge, *Charger*'s crew immediately ordered the carrier's engines stopped and executed a full left rudder then a full right rudder to avoid Behrens's downed aircraft. Unfortunately for Behrens, *Charger* could not turn on a dime. She struck the downed aircraft, forcing it to sink. At 1003, the plane guard U.S. Coast Guard cutter *CGC83369* recovered ENS Behrens. He was immediately transferred to *Charger* and rushed to Sick Bay for medical attention. Eleven minutes later, *Charger* resumed flight operations. At 1210 just over two hours after the mishap, *Charger*'s Medical Officer LT E. N. Davie Jr. pronounced ENS

---

[67] U.S. Navy. *USS Charger.* CVE-30. Deck Log. January 1943. RG38, NARA, Archives II. See entries for 2- 6 January 1943.

Behrens deceased. That night *CGC83369* transported his body back to Naval Operating Base Norfolk.[68]

ENS Behrens's crash was not the only mishap that day. At 1603, ENS R. W. Cummings was attempting to land a TBF-1 Avenger. He caught the Number Five arresting wire but his Avenger's tail hook broke, sending the aircraft careening into *Charger*'s island. The impact tore the aircraft's starboard wing off. The Avenger then struck the starboard catwalk. One of its landing gear caught on the catwalk, which prevented the aircraft from going over the side and into the water.[69]

The next day, ENS Edmund Seradjuan missed the arresting wires while landing his SNJ trainer aircraft and crashed into the barrier. The pilot was uninjured and the SNJ was slightly damaged.[70]

Charger did not have another aviation mishap until 22 January. On that day at 1128, Sub-Lieutenant R. C. E. Hutchinson of the Royal Navy attempted to land his F4F Wildcat aboard the training carrier. He missed the arresting wires, crashed through the barrier and went over the side into the water off the port bow. Again, the crew of the ship's bridge reacted immediately. They ordered the engines stopped then steered around the Wildcat which sank shortly thereafter. The plane was lost but Sub-Lieutenant

---

[68] U.S. Navy. *USS Charger.* CVE-30. Deck Log. January 1943. RG38, NARA, Archives II. See Entry for 12 January 1943.

[69] U.S. Navy. *USS Charger.* CVE-30. Deck Log. January 1943. RG38, NARA, Archives II. See Entry for 12 January 1943.

[70] U.S. Navy. *USS Charger.* CVE-30. Deck Log. January 1943. RG38, NARA, Archives II. See Entry for 13 January 1943.

Hutchinson was rescued by *CGC83369* having suffered only minor abrasions.[71]

Four days later, another Royal Navy had a serious mishap aboard *Charger.* Sub-Lieutenant R. C. Wilkinson missed the arresting wires, crashed into the barrier and flipped over his F4F Wildcat. Wilkinson suffered minor lacerations but his aircraft was severely damaged.[72]

On 28 January 1943, *Charger* got underway for Naval Operating Base Norfolk. At 1050, the ship suffered a steering casualty and control was shifted to the after steering station. Fifteen minutes later, she anchored and repairs were made. At 1258, she got underway again but suffered another steering control casualty. Again, control was shifted to the after steering station. At 1309, the ship stopped and anchored so that repairs could be made. The next morning, *Charger* got underway again and again suffered a steering casualty. She managed to get back to Naval Operating Base Norfolk and repairs commenced again.[73]

1943 had not started out well. *Charger* had conducted flight operations on twenty-one of January's thirty-one days. ENS Gordon Behrens died in the crash of his FM2 Wildcat. Two *Charger* enlisted sailors had been injured on New Year's Day by an arresting wire that had parted. There had been ten aviation

---

[71] U.S. Navy. *USS Charger.* CVE-30. Deck Log. January 1943. RG38, NARA, Archives II. See Entry for 22 January 1943.

[72] U.S. Navy. *USS Charger.* CVE-30. Deck Log. January 1943. RG38, NARA, Archives II. See Entry for 26 January 1943.

[73] U.S. Navy. *USS Charger.* CVE-30. Deck Log. January 1943. RG38, NARA, Archives II. See Entries for 28 to 31 January 1943.

mishaps that month with three aircraft lost in the Chesapeake Bay. Then while returning to NOB Norfolk, *Charger* suffered several steering casualties.[74]

During the month of February 1943, *Charger* conducted flight operations on ten of the month's twenty-eight days. She spent the first seven days of February pier side, then cast off on 8 February and headed for the operational training area. She concluded flight operations on 18 February and returned to Naval Operating Base Norfolk where she remained for the duration of February.[75]

Charger experienced six aviation mishaps during February 1943. Fortunately, there were no fatalities and only one minor injury. On 11 February, ENS George M. Cohan's F4F Wildcat broke its right landing gear while landing. In addition to the broken landing gear, the aircraft damaged its propeller. Five days later, ENS J. M. Bristo missed the arresting wires and crashed into the starboard catwalk. His SB2U-1 Vought Vindicator dive-bomber suffered major damage but he escaped with only minor injuries. The other four mishaps all occurred on 17 February. At 1317, ENS R. Burns caught the number two arresting wire but slid into the port catwalk. His Vindicator sustained minor damage. At 1517, ENS G. S. Beckham was taking off from *Charger* in a SB2U Vindicator when he applied the brakes, thus nosing his aircraft over and damaging its propeller. At 1701, ENS Hugh McLinden caught the Number Five arresting wire but rolled his Vindicator into the port catwalk.

---

[74] U.S. Navy. *USS Charger.* CVE-30. Deck Log. January 1943. RG38, NARA, Archives II.

[75] U.S. Navy. *USS Charger.* CVE-30. Deck Log. February 1943. RG38. NARA, Archives II.

Finally at 1838, ENS James Douthit was landing a TBF Avenger when he struck the port catwalk.[76]

March 1943 was a very busy month for *USS Charger*. Flight operations were conducted on seventeen days that month. *Charger* also experienced eleven aviation mishaps that month and had problems with its port main engine that required repairs while in the operating area. Fog suspended flight operations on 6 March and 19 March. Heavy snowfall and limited visibility halted flight operations on 22 March.[77]

There were four minor mishaps aboard *Charger* during the first cycle of flight operations in March. Three of these occurred on 7 March. The day seemed to begin well enough. At 1114, ENS R. Valencia landed aboard in the Navy's new Grumman F6F-3 Hellcat fighter, and ultimately completed eight qualification landings. The first mishap occurred at 1223. LT(jg) Marvin L. Leedom caught the Number Six arresting wire but his TBF-1 Avenger rolled into the port catwalk. Then at 1440, another TBF-1 Avenger piloted by ENS James L. Sweetser caught the Number Eight arresting wire but afterwards brushed the island with his starboard wing. Lastly at 1706, ENS Charles A. Enight crashed into the barrier while attempting to land a SB2U-1 Vindicator bomber. Then the following day, ENS K. T. Kerr crashed his F4F Wildcat into the barrier. [78]

---

[76] U.S. Navy. *USS Charger.* CVE-30. Deck Log. February 1943. RG38, NARA, Archives II.

[77] U.S. Navy. *USS Charger.* CVE-30. Deck Log. March 1943. RG38, NARA, Archives II.

[78] U.S. Navy. *USS Charger.* CVE-30. Deck Log. March 1943. RG38, NARA, Archives II. See Entry for 7 March 1943.

Charger was at NOB Norfolk from 11 to 14 March. On 15 March, *Charger* was transferred from Task Group 31.2 to Task Unit 21.9.2. Her mission of training pilots remained the same. Flight operations resumed and 2ndLt F. G. Coffman, USMCR, crashed his F4F Wildcat into *Charger*'s bridge. Surprisingly there were no injuries and only minor damage to the aircraft. On 16 March, ENS John D. Morrison missed the arresting wires and crashed his TBF-1 Avenger into the port catwalk. Fortunately, there were no injuries.[79]

On 18 March, *Charger* was used for carrier aviation experiments. CAPT C. A. Bulster, USN, and an observer team from the Navy Bureau of Aeronautics came aboard.   At 1152, LCDR L. C. Simpler, USN, landed a modified F4F-3 Wildcat.   He then performed three jet-assisted take-offs with his Wildcat.[80]

Charger resumed regular flight operations. Fog halted operations on 19 April and a snowstorm cancelled flight operations on 22 March. There were four aviation mishaps on 23 March. At 0812 ENS John P. Pearson crashed a F4F Wildcat into the barrier. About an hour later, ENS Milan S. Nemsals caught the Number Nine wire but still crashed his TBF-1 Avenger into the barrier. Less than an hour after that, ENS Alonzo C. Hall had a barrier crash with his SBD-4 Dauntless dive-bomber. Lastly, ENS Richard J. Walsh

---

[79] U.S. Navy. *USS Charger.* CVE-30. Deck Log. March 1943. RG38, NARA, Archives II.

[80] U.S. Navy. *USS Charger.* CVE-30. Deck Log. March 1943. RG38, NARA, Archives II.

caught the Number 2 arresting wire but still hit the port catwalk. His TBF-1 Avenger sustained major damage.[81]

28 March was noteworthy for two occurrences. On a positive note, ENS E. Delanez performed the 10,000th landing aboard *Charger* at 0812 that day. He was piloting a TBF-1 Avenger at the time. On the negative side, ENS J. M. Lewis became the 11th pilot to suffer a mishap on *Charger* that month when he crashed a F4F Wildcat into the port catwalk. His Wildcat suffered serious damage.[82]

Navy Fighting Squadron VF-17 and *Charger*

LCDR Tom Blackburn was back aboard *Charger* in March 1943, this time as commanding officer of Navy Fighting Squadron VF-17, nicknamed "the Jolly Rogers." Their insignia was the Skull and Crossbones reminiscent of pirate flags. Their new F4U Corsairs were larger, heavier and much faster than the F4F Wildcats that Blackburn had previously brought aboard *Charger* for carrier qualifications. On 8 March 1943, Blackburn attempted to qualify. His first actual carrier landing with a Corsair was very eventful. The Corsair had a long nose which made seeing the small carrier difficult on the landing approach. Blackburn hit the deck hard, bouncing high but catching an arresting wire. The impact blew out both of his main tires, but fortunately there was no other damage. "My next four touchdowns and arrests – all I needed to

---

[81] U.S. Navy. *USS Charger.* CVE-30. Deck Log. March 1943. RG38, NARA, Archives II.

[82] U.S. Navy. *USS Charger.* CVE-30. Deck Log. March 1943. RG38, NARA, Archives II.

qualify for carrier ops in a Corsair – were not as exciting," Blackburn would later write in his memoirs.[83]

Apparently someone aboard *Charger* deemed LCDR Blackburn's return to the carrier as noteworthy. The following entry was later added to the ship's Deck Log:

> 1431 Lt. Comdr. C. T. Blackburn, USN, landed aboard in F4U -1 airplane Bu. No.02340 (17-F-6) commencing a series of four qualification landings which were completed successfully at 1745.

The entry was attested to by the ship's navigator, LCDR R. W. Allen, USN.[84]

Most of Blackburn's pilots had never landed aboard a carrier before. "Moreover, *Charger* hardly qualified as a carrier; that spitkit rarely produced the 25 knots of relative wind over her flight deck that was considered the standard minimum for safe landing operations." On his landing attempt, one of Blackburn's pilots -- Ensign Jack Chasnoff -- bounced his Corsair higher than the ship's masthead, an experience that convinced him to forego any further landing attempts. Instead he flew his plane back to Naval Air Station Norfolk. "VF-17 got through carrier qualifications with no personnel casualties. We busted a lot of wheels, blew a lot of tires,

---

[83] Blackburn, pp. 44-5.; U.S. Navy. *USS Charger.* CVE-30. Deck Log. March 1943. RG38, NARA, Archives II.

[84] U.S. Navy. *USS Charger.* CVE-30. Deck Log. March 1943. RG38, NARA, Archives II. See Entry Addenda for 8 March 1943.

and totaled several of our airplanes, but everyone eventually made his five qualifying landings aboard *Charger*."[85]

After earning their carrier qualifications aboard *Charger*, the pilots of VF-17 were assigned to the *Essex*-class fleet carrier *USS Bunker Hill* (CV-17). In the midst of their deployment aboard *Bunker Hill*, the Navy determined that F4U Corsairs were not safe to operate from carriers. So VF-17 was removed from *Bunker Hill* and replaced by the F6F Hellcats of VF-18. VF-17 instead operated from land bases in the Solomon Islands. During six months of combat, the pilots of VF-17 shot down an astounding 154.5 Japanese aircraft; thirteen of its pilots became aces. Blackburn himself shot down 13 of those aircraft and earned the Navy Cross for his exploits. The squadron was disbanded in 1944 but several of the pilots, including squadron executive officer LCDR Roger Hedrick, formed the nucleus of a new fighter squadron - VF-84 - which did operate from *Bunker Hill* in 1945.[86]

Spring 1943

Flight operations for *Charger* in April 1943 did not start until the fifth day of the month. On 6 April, LT R. M. Swensson USN caught an arresting wire but still crashed his TBF-1 Avenger into the port catwalk. The next day, ENS D. C. McGaughlin had a barrier crash with a SNJ-3 trainer. Two days later, ENS Edwin Free crashed into the barrier. He was not injured but one of

---

85 Blackburn, pp. 44-5.

86 See Blackburn's memoirs *The Jolly Rogers: The Story of Tom Blackburn and Navy Fighting Squadron VF-17* for more details. Interestingly enough, my great uncle (on my father's side) LT(jg) James A. Nist was a pilot in VF-84.

Charger's barrier tenders, Seaman 1st Class Thomas E. O'Donnell suffered a compound fracture to his right tibia.[87]

On 10 April, *Charger* experienced its second fatal aviation mishap of the year. While attempting to land, LT(jg) W. R. Livegey lost control of his SNJ-3C and went into the water. One of *Charger's* plane guards *CGC83319* searched for the pilot while the carrier continued flight operations. LT(jg) Livegey was not found.[88]

From 11 April to 13 April, *Charger* performed shipboard training exercises. This included day and night battle practice, torpedo defense and anti-aircraft defense.[89]

Flight operations resumed on the morning of 13 April. ENS Frank G. Smith crashed his SB2U2 dive-bomber into the barrier. Flight operations concluded at 1252 and *Charger* returned to NOB Norfolk.[90]

On 19 April, *Charger* got underway and returned to the operating area. Unfortunately, fog and periodic rain prevented flight operations that day, so *Charger* anchored and waited for the weather to improve. The following day, the weather improved sufficiently to conduct flight operations. Flight operations were

---

[87] U.S. Navy. *USS Charger.* CVE-30. Deck Log. April 1943. RG38, NARA, Archives II.

[88] U.S. Navy. *USS Charger.* CVE-30. Deck Log. April 1943. RG38, NARA, Archives II. See Entry for 10 April 1943.

[89] U.S. Navy. *USS Charger.* CVE-30. Deck Log. April 1943. RG38, NARA, Archives II.

[90] U.S. Navy. *USS Charger.* CVE-30. Deck Log. April 1943. RG38, NARA, Archives II.

conducted on seven of the next eight days. At 1145 on 25 April, ENS R. K. Burke's TBF-1 Avenger experienced an engine failure. Burke performed a water landing. His plane sank immediately but he was rescued by one of the plane guard Coast Guard cutters. On 26 April, the ship also performed torpedo defense and anti-aircraft defense drills.[91]

Also on 26 April, *Charger* experienced a engineering casualty to its port main engine. Flight operations were halted while repairs were performed. Apparently the cause of the casualty was a broken water hose. Repairs were affected and flight operations were resumed. Two days later, *Charger* concluded its flight operations for the month and returned to Naval Operating Base Norfolk.[92]

May 1943 began with *Charger* tied to a pier at NOB Norfolk. Repairs were performed on the troublesome port main engine between 4 May and 7 May. She then moved to the anchorage in Hampton Roads and remained there until 11 May. Later that month, CDR Thomas A. Ahroon was promoted to become the ship's Executive Officer.[93]

---

[91] U.S. Navy. *USS Charger.* CVE-30. Deck Log. April 1943. RG38, NARA, Archives II.

[92] U.S. Navy. *USS Charger.* CVE-30. Deck Log. April 1943. RG38, NARA, Archives II.

[93] U.S. Navy. *USS Charger.* CVE-30. Deck Log. May 1943. RG38, NARA, Archives II.; U.S. Navy. Office of Information. Biographies Branch. "Rear Admiral Thomas A. Ahroon – United States Navy." 31 March 1960.

On the morning of 11 May, *Charger* left the Hampton Roads anchorage and proceeded up the Chesapeake Bay to her regular operating area. Thereafter followed seven days of flight operations. Five aviation mishaps occurred during this period. Two mishaps involving TBF Avengers occurred on 13 May 1943. First, 2ndLt B. M. Radcliffe, USMCR crashed into the port catwalk. Then, ENS V. A. Bergeson crashed into the port catwalk. There were no injuries in either mishap and both aircraft sustained only minor damage. The next day, ENS Earl W. Smith crashed a SNJ into the starboard catwalk. ENS Rector had a barrier crash in a SB2C Helldiver on 15 May and LT(jg) P. E. Johnson crashed into the barrier with a Helldiver two days later. Flight operations were concluded on 17 May and the ship returned to NOB Norfolk.[94]

The port main engine proved troublesome again. On three of the six nights that *Charger* was in the operating area, the port main engine had to be taken out of commission for repairs.[95]

Charger went back to the operating area on 24 May. Starting on 25 May, she conducted seven days of flight operations. There were three more aviation mishaps. ENS L. Hill crashed an SNJ into the port catwalk on 25 May. LT J. M. Bunneston of the Royal Navy caught Number 3 arresting wire but still crashed his TBF Avenger into the port catwalk on 27 May. There were no injuries and only slight damage to the aircraft. LT(jg) J. R. Dunn had a barrier crash with a SB2C-1 Helldiver on 29 May. The troublesome port main

---

[94] U.S. Navy. *USS Charger.* CVE-30. Deck Log. May 1943. RG38, NARA, Archives II.

[95] U.S. Navy. *USS Charger.* CVE-30. Deck Log. May 1943. RG38, NARA, Archives II.

engine had to be taken out of commission for repairs on five nights.[96]

During the month of May, *Charger* conducted flight operations on fourteen days and there were eight aviation mishaps but fortunately no injuries and serious damage to aircraft. The ship was continually plagued with problems with its port main engine.[97]

June 1943 was another troublesome month for *USS Charger.* On a positive note, *Charger* passed her annual military inspection. The ship's annual military inspection was performed by CAPT Greer, commanding officer of *USS Core* (CVE-13). There were two aviation mishaps during the month of June 1943. At 0940 on 1 June 1943, LT N. E. Peterson caught the Number Three wire but still crashed his F6F-3 Hellcat into the port catwalk. At 0802 on 4 June, LT(jg) S. R. Cumming crashed into the barrier with an SNJ. Fortunately, neither mishap caused any injuries. Flight operations were limited due to repeated problems with the port engine. On 2 June 1943, the port engine went out of commission, requiring repairs. Further repairs were required on 5 June. On 18 June, *Charger* went into the Norfolk Navy Yard for repairs.[98]

Charger spent the remainder of June and the entire month of July 1943 at the Norfolk Navy Yard. On 7 July, she went into Drydock Number 4. At 2025, the Navy Yard workers commenced pumping

---

[96] U.S. Navy. *USS Charger.* CVE-30. Deck Log. May 1943. RG38, NARA, Archives II.

[97] U.S. Navy. *USS Charger.* CVE-30. Deck Log. May 1943. RG38, NARA, Archives II.

[98] U.S. Navy. *USS Charger.* CVE-30. Deck Log. June 1943. RG38, NARA, Archives II.

out the drydock and by 2330, the ship was resting on keel blocks. Her sister ship *USS Card* (CVE-11) was sharing the drydock with her. The following day, *Charger*'s Engineer Officer examined all outboard valves connected to the Engineering Department and pronounced them satisfactory. The ship's First Lieutenant examined all other outboard valves, the rudder and all other underwater fittings and pronounced them satisfactory. Propeller 2B was replaced with a modified one to reduce vibration. On 12 July at 0440, flooding of Drydock Number 4 commenced. When completed, both *Charger* and *Card* left drydock with the assistance of tugboats and moved to pier side berths. At 1355, a Navy Yard floating crane came alongside *Charger* for the installation of a catapult. This being accomplished, the crane cast off at 1600. On 30 July at 1344, a Navy Yard painter, Charles Raleigh Fulgham, was struck in the head by a 2 foot by 12 foot plank that fell from overhead on the Quarterdeck. He was quickly taken by ambulance to the Navy Yard Dispensary for treatment for a scalp laceration, brain concussion and shock.[99]

USS Charger finally left the Norfolk Navy Yard on 2 August 1943. She conducted post-repair trials, and then the following day, underwent magnetic degaussing. Degaussing was the process which used electricity to reduce or eliminate a ship's magnetic field. Doing so, help reduce or eliminate the ship's vulnerability to magnetic anti-ship mines.[100]

---

[99] U.S. Navy. *USS Charger.* CVE-30. Deck Log. July 1943. RG38, NARA, Archives II.

[100] U.S. Navy. *USS Charger.* CVE-30. Deck Log. August 1943. RG38, NARA, Archives II.

It would appear that *Charger* attempted to make up for lost time in the Navy Yard. She conducted flight operations on twenty-three days in August. There eleven aviation mishaps that month. Eight of the August mishaps were minor affairs with minimal damage to aircraft and minor or no injuries to personnel. On 12 August, ENS M. E. Nobles crashed a F6F Hellcat into the port catwalk. On 22 August, LT C. V. Timberlake had a barrier crash with a SNJ4C trainer aircraft. On 25 August, the right landing gear on LT(jg) W. Roach's SBD-3 Dauntless dive bomber buckled while landing. That same day, ENS T. E. Jenkins and ENS J. H. Doane both had barrier crashes with SNJ3Cs. On 27 August at 1632, LT J. J. Collins crashed into the barrier with a SNJ3C. 27 August was not LT Collins's day. A half hour after crashing that SNJ3C into the barrier, LT Collins crashed into the barrier again with a different SNJ3C. This second time, however, he had caught an arresting wire but the tail hook had failed, sending him into the barrier. The next day, ENS Kennard King had a barrier crash with a TBF-1 Avenger. The final mishap of the month occurred when ENS L. J. Miller nosed over a SBD-5 Dauntless while preparing for take-off.[101]

There were also three mishaps that resulted in either aircraft being lost or personnel injuries or both. At 1732 on 8 August, the F4F-4 Wildcat piloted by ENS G. T. Wilkinson missed the arresting wires and struck the upper portion of the barrier with its landing gear. Wilkinson's Wildcat then crashed over the bow and into the water. ENS Wilkinson was rescued by U.S. Coast Guard Cutter *CGC 88324* which was serving as plane guard. His Wildcat, however, was not recovered. At 1855 on 24 August, ENS D. N. Rose was

---

[101] U.S. Navy. *USS Charger.* CVE-30. Deck Log. August 1943. RG38, NARA, Archives II.

circling a SBD-3 Dauntless when he crashed into the water at Latitude 37 degrees 19 minutes 3 seconds North, Longitude 76 degrees 9 minutes West or about 43 miles from Wolf Trap Light. He was rescued and treated for lacerations to his face and multiple contusions and abrasions. The plane was not recovered.[102]

The most serious aviation mishap of the month occurred at 1344 on 14 August. While attempting to land a F6F Hellcat, LT C. W. Harbert crashed into the after searchlight platform and ramp of the flight deck. The plane was severely damaged and the pilot sustained contusions to his left shoulder and abrasions on his chest. The ship's company, however, suffered much greater. Several *Charger* sailors were in the vicinity of Harbert's crash. Baker 2nd Class Samuel Lee suffered a compound fracture of his right lower leg and right foot. Ship's Cook 2nd Class Wilburn D. Tatum suffered a fracture of his right ankle and lacerations to the back of his head. Seaman 2nd Class Russell Wilburn, Motor Machinists Mate 1st Class Anthony Farrugio, Fireman 3rd Class Beufard H. Winters, Seaman 2nd Class T. A. Smith, Jr. and Boatswains Mate (Canvasman) 2nd Class William H. Kettle all suffered a variety of contusions, lacerations, and abrasions.[103]

Charger was plagued by intermittent problems with her port engine throughout September 1943. For example, on 10

---

[102] U.S. Navy. *USS Charger.* CVE-30. Deck Log. August 1943. RG38, NARA, Archives II.

[103] U.S. Navy. *USS Charger.* CVE-30. Deck Log. August 1943. RG38, NARA, Archives II.

September, a leak in the fuel valve forced a shut down of the port engine so that necessary repairs could be made.[104]

Despite her recurring port engine problems, *Charger* conducted flight operations on seventeen days in September. On 10 September 1943, LCDR Avery performed the first night landing aboard *Charger.* Twelve mishaps occurred though only one resulted in the loss of an aircraft. On 1 September, ENS P. M. Charton nosed his SNJ-4C over during take-off. ENS H. H. Watson crashed a SBD-5 Dauntless into the barrier on 10 September. On 13 September, LT(jg) D. C. Puckett crashed a F4F-4 Wildcat into the barrier. On 24 September, ENS E. L. Childers and LT(jg) Laur had barrier crashes with TBF Avengers. There were three mishaps on 27 September. LCDR H. P. Allingham of the Royal Navy crashed a F4U Corsair into the barrier. LT(jg) F. M. Roundtrea had a barrier crash with a TBF-1 Avenger. LT(jg) C. G. Hewitt's TBF1-C Avenger suffered a landing gear collapse when he attempted to land aboard *Charger.* There were two barrier crashes on 29 September. LCDR H. P. Allingham crashed another F4U Corsair into the barrier. Seaman 2nd Class R. Carr suffered a minor cut over his left eye in the mishap. ENS J. H. Steward crashed a FM-1 Wildcat into the barrier. The most serious mishap of the month occurred on 12 September. At 1250, ENS T. J. Wadsworth took off from *Charger* in a F4F Wildcat. He failed to gain sufficient altitude and crashed into the water. ENS Wadsworth was rescued; his Wildcat was not.

---

[104] U.S. Navy. *USS Charger.* CVE-30. Deck Log. September 1943. RG38, NARA, Archives II.

Flight operations were cancelled on 30 September due to winds in excess of 60 knots and intermittent rain.[105]

The month of October 1943 was a combination of routine operations and unique occurrences. *Charger* conducted flight operations on fourteen days, experienced six aviation mishaps, celebrated its 16,000th carrier landing, visited the U.S. Naval Academy at Annapolis, experienced a civilian injury aboard and had her main engines worked on at the Norfolk Navy Yard. *Charger* began the month with a visit from the tug *Bomezee*. The tug came alongside towing a lighter. *Charger* then transferred two damaged aircraft to the lighter. Later that day, *Charger* steamed north and anchored off Annapolis, Maryland. She remained anchored there until the morning of 4 October, then headed south to resume flight operations. That same day, ENS J. H. Drew broke his Avenger's tail hook while attempting to land, sending him and his aircraft into the crash barrier. Later that day, LT(jg) H. V. Ladley missed the arresting wires and then went through the crash barrier. He and his F6F Hellcat then went over the side and into the water off the port bow. *CGC 83368* promptly rescued LT(jg) Ladley but his Hellcat remained a long term guest of the Chesapeake Bay. Two days later, ENS R. H. Zehgen successfully landed a SBD Dauntless, thus making *Charger*'s 16,000th carrier landing. On 14 October, LT John McGree crashed a TBF-1C into the barrier. Fog and rain shortened flight operations on 16 October and cancelled them completely on 26 October. On 17 October, the tail hook on ENS R. F. Browning's F4F Wildcat snapped upon landing, sending him and his plane into the barrier. Also that day,

---

[105] U.S. Navy. *USS Charger.* CVE-30. Deck Log. September 1943. RG38, NARA, Archives II.; U.S. Navy. *USS Charger.* CVE-30 History of *USS Charger* (CVE-30). 24 May 1945. RG38. NARA. Archives II. [Hereafter cited as *Charger* History.] page 2.

ENS A. M. DeCesaro crashed a SBD-5 Dauntless into the port catwalk. The final mishap of the month occurred on 30 October when ENS A. W. Yardarogh crashed a TBF-1C Avenger into the port catwalk. *Charger* was back at the Norfolk Navy Yard on several days of repairs to the main engines. On 20 October, a civilian rigger Norman L. Starling fell off a ladder while working in the Hangar Deck. He sustained a compound fracture of the left ankle and was taken to the Navy Yard Dispensary for treatment.[106]

CDR Thomas A. Ahroon left *USS Charger* in October 1943. He had been with *Charger* since February 1942, assisting with her fitting out, and serving as first her Air Officer and then her Executive Officer. His next assignment was to fit out another escort carrier, *USS White Plains* (CVE-66).[107]

During November 1943, *Charger* conducted flight operations on nineteen days, experienced ten aviation mishaps and had a Change of Command. On 1 November, LT(jg) Norman T. Dowty crashed a TBM-1C Avenger into the barrier. The following day, ENS F. Hancock repeated the feat with a F6F Hellcat. Three days later, LT D. W. Mulcahy caught the Number One arresting wire but still crashed his Hellcat into the port catwalk. Fortunately, the damage was minor. On 12 November, Royal Navy Sub-Lieutenant Dickson also crashed into the port catwalk after catching an arresting wire. He was piloting a TBF Avenger at the time. Not long after, Sub-Lieutenant D. R. Whitehead crashed into the barrier after the tail hook on his Avenger sheered off. The next day, Sub-

---

[106] U.S. Navy. *USS Charger.* CVE-30. Deck Log. October 1943. RG38, NARA, Archives II.

[107] U.S. Navy. Office of Information. Biographies Branch. "Rear Admiral Thomas A. Ahroon – United States Navy." 31 March 1960.

Lieutenant M. T. Blair caught the Number Six wire but still crashed his F4U Corsair into the starboard catwalk. Later that day, the tail hook of LT(jg) C. S. Longano's SNJ snapped off while landing, sending him and his aircraft into the barrier. On 29 November, damaged F4U Corsair Number 18002 and F6F Hellcat Number 26049 were taken off the ship for repairs.[108]

Three of the month's aviation mishaps resulted in the loss of aircraft. The two of these mishaps both occurred on 22 November. LT Donald Chute of the Royal Navy crashed over the starboard side while attempting to land. He was rescued by *CGC 83475*. Later that day, LT R. E. Rice crashed his SBD Dauntless into the water on takeoff and *CGC 83475* made its second rescue of the day. Both planes were lost. The most serious aviation mishap of the month occurred on 5 November. At approximately 0818, ENS Ivan Acton Edwards was attempting to land a F6F Hellcat aboard *Charger*. He caught the Number Three wire but the tail assembly broke, splitting the plane in two. ENS Edwards and the forward section of the Hellcat crashed into the port catwalk and went over the side into the water. The plane sank immediately. The plane guard Coast Guard cutters searched in vain for the pilot. Flying debris from the Hellcat struck two *Charger* sailors. Seaman 2nd Class Joseph P. Samsel suffered slight contusions and abrasions to his left knee. Aviation Machinists Mate 3rd Class Donald W. House suffered a fracture to his left leg.[109]

---

[108] U.S. Navy. *USS Charger*. CVE-30. Deck Log. November 1943. RG38, NARA, Archives II.

[109] U.S. Navy. *USS Charger*. CVE-30. Deck Log. November 1943. RG38, NARA, Archives II.

On 6 November 1943, *Charger* said good-bye to its commanding officer and welcomed a new one to command. CAPT Grover B. H. Hall remained in command of *Charger* until 6 November 1943. During his time in command, *Charger* performed approximately 11,000 landings. He was relieved by CAPT Ralph W. D. Woods. CAPT Hall then became the Director of the Naval Research Laboratory at Naval Station Anacostia, Washington DC.[110]

Like Hall, CAPT Ralph W. D. Woods was a graduate of the U.S. Naval Academy. A member of the Class of '23, Woods was two years behind Hall at Annapolis. CAPT Woods had a long and distinguished career in naval aviation. Born on 4 May 1902 in Chicago, Illinois, Woods attended the U.S. Naval Academy and graduated with the Class of 1923. He was a plank-owner of the new battleship *USS West Virginia* (BB-48) and also served aboard the battleship *USS Arkansas* (BB-33). He attended flight school at NAS Pensacola and earned his wings in November 1927. One of his Pensacola classmates Ernest J. King would later become Commander-in-Chief of the U.S. Fleet during World War Two. During the 1930s, he served aboard *Saratoga, Lexington* and *Ranger.* While serving with Scouting Squadron 2B on *Saratoga,* he participated in the search for the missing aviators Amelia Earhart and Fred Noonan in July 1937. He commanded Scouting Squadron 42 on *Ranger* from January 1939 to June 1940. CAPT Woods participated in the November 1942 invasion of North Africa

---

[110] U.S. Navy. *USS Charger.* CVE-30. Deck Log. November 1943. RG38, NARA, Archives II.; U.S. Navy. *USS Charger.* CVE-30 History of *USS Charger* (CVE-30). 24 May 1945. RG38. NARA. Archives II. [Hereafter cited as *Charger* History.]

as a staff officer with Amphibious Force – Atlantic Fleet. CAPT Woods took *Charger* out for the first time on 8 November.[111]

During the month of December 1943, *Charger* conducted flight operations on sixteen days, contended with poor weather conditions which hindered flight operations on several days and experienced major problems with its arresting gear system.[112]

The month of December 1943 began poorly. On 1 December, VF-14 was performing carrier qualifications. Only eighteen landings had occurred when the Number Four arresting cable snapped, whipping across the flight deck. Three enlisted men of the flight deck crew were struck by the cable and seriously injured. *Charger* immediately halted flight operations and proceeded at full speed for Naval Operating Base Norfolk. Upon arriving there, the injured sailors were transferred ashore and taken to the Norfolk Naval Hospital for treatment. As the War Diary recorded, "It was strongly recommended that the purchase cables of the first three arresting gear units be renewed with 11/16-inch wire before operations be resumed. These cables have been engaged by landing aircraft 2381; 4316; 5471; times respectively since originally installed."[113]

---

[111] Ralph W. D. Woods Veteran Tribute http://www.veterantributes.org/TributeDetail.php?recordID=990; U.S. Navy. *USS Charger.* CVE-30. Deck Log. November 1943. RG38, NARA, Archives II.

[112] U.S. Navy. USS Charger. CVE-30. War Diary for December 1943. 1 January 1944. RG38, NARA, Archives II. Note: The National Archives holdings switched from Deck Logs to monthly War Diaries for *Charger* in this month.

[113] U.S. Navy. USS Charger. CVE-30. War Diary for December 1943. 1 January 1944. RG38, NARA, Archives II.

Nevertheless, *Charger* went back to the operating area. She performed nine landings on 2 December and another twenty-four landings on 3 December. There was one barrier crash. Thick fog and poor visibility cancelled flight operations for 4 December.[114]

On 6-7 December, *Charger* was at the Norfolk Navy Yard for much needed repairs to the arresting gear system. "The purchase cables on the first three arresting gear assemblies renewed and other minor repairs and alterations being accomplished by the Navy Yard personnel," recorded the War Diary.[115]

After two days in the Navy Yard, *Charger* returned to the operating area for flight operations. Fifty-three landings were performed by VF(N)-75 and VF-9.[116]

On 9 December, RADM Jesse B. Oldendorf came aboard to observe flight operations. VF(N)-75 obliged him, performing 23 landings. A 1909 graduate of USNA, Oldendorf had a distinguished career in the surface Navy that included tours as Executive Officer of the battleship *USS West Virginia* (BB-48) and command of the cruiser *USS Houston* (CA-30). During World War Two, he served as Commander Trinidad Sector, Caribbean Sea Frontier and Commandant of Naval Operating Base, Trinidad, from 2 July, 1942 to April 19, 1943. Then he commanded a task

---

[114] U.S. Navy. USS Charger. CVE-30. War Diary for December 1943. 1 January 1944. RG38, NARA, Archives II.

[115] U.S. Navy. USS Charger. CVE-30. War Diary for December 1943. 1 January 1944. RG38, NARA, Archives II.

[116] U.S. Navy. USS Charger. CVE-30. War Diary for December 1943. 1 January 1944. RG38, NARA, Archives II.

force of the Atlantic Fleet from 2 May 1943 to 25 November 1943.[117]

On 10 December, *Charger* welcomed aboard Navy Fleet Composite Squadron Fifty-Eight (VC-58). Organized for service aboard escort carriers, VC squadrons were previously known as Auxiliary Scout Squadrons (VGS). Like their predecessors, VC squadrons were equipped with fighters and bombers, usually FM-2 or F4F Wildcats and TBF or TBM Avengers. Fifteen VC-58 pilots performed 46 landings, then were instructed in catapult launches. After receiving instruction, the fifteen pilots experienced catapult launches with their aircraft.[118]

Landings and instruction in catapult launches continued on 11 December when seventeen pilots were trained in the latter. On 12 December, VF-14 pilots performed 112 landings without a mishap but the following day, an aircraft crashed into the catwalk, causing heavy damage to the aircraft and minor injuries to the pilot. Flight operations were severely hampered by fog and low visibility on 14 December. Only thirty-six landings were accomplished. The fog and visibility were so bad that flight operations were cancelled

---

[117] U.S. Navy. USS Charger. CVE-30. War Diary for December 1943. 1 January 1944. RG38, NARA, Archives II.; "Jesse Barrett Oldendorf 16 February 1887 - 27 April 1974." U.S. Naval History and Heritage Command. Accessed online on 10 September 2020 at https://www.history.navy.mil/research/library/research-guides/modern-biographical-files-ndl/modern-bios-o/oldendorf-jesse-barrett.html

[118] U.S. Navy. USS Charger. CVE-30. War Diary for December 1943. 1 January 1944. RG38, NARA, Archives II.

altogether on 15 December and the ship returned to NOB Norfolk.[119]

Two days later, *Charger* was back on station training pilots. VN-15 and VFW-76 performed 109 landings that day. Only 28 landings were performed the following day but the ship conducted night battle practice, firing off 3-inch star shells and 5-inch live ammunition. Flight operations were cancelled on the morning of 19 December due to fog and low visibility. Thirty-five landings were performed in the afternoon and the ship practiced 20mm gunnery, expending 1,124 rounds. Over the next three days, five squadrons conducted 356 landings.[120]

Flight operations for the month and the year concluded on 22 December. On 24 December, sailors from *USS Guadalcanal* (CVE-60) conducted damage control practice aboard *Charger* while sailors from *Charger* did the same training aboard *USS Humboldt* (AVP-21). On Christmas Day, *Charger* moored to Pier #5 at the Norfolk Navy Yard. For the rest of December 1943, workers from the navy yard performed modifications to the structure of *Charger*'s bridge and various other repairs and modifications to the ship.[121]

---

[119] U.S. Navy. USS Charger. CVE-30. War Diary for December 1943. 1 January 1944. RG38, NARA, Archives II.

[120] U.S. Navy. USS Charger. CVE-30. War Diary for December 1943. 1 January 1944. RG38, NARA, Archives II.

[121] U.S. Navy. USS Charger. CVE-30. War Diary for December 1943. 1 January 1944. RG38, NARA, Archives II.

Chapter Six
ENS Ralph A. Thibodeau, USNR

[Author's Note: I am grateful to ENS (later LT) Thibodeau's son Ralph Jr. for providing me with a biography of his late father. This chapter based primarily on his biography with several additional sources where noted.]

As was typical for Navy ships in World War Two, *USS Charger* contained a diverse group of men from all across the United States. One such individual was the ship's Landing Signal Officer, ENS Ralph A. Thibodeau of Faribault, Minnesota.

Ralph A. Thibodeau was born on 4 August 1921 in Faribault, Minnesota. Faribault was a small city in southeastern Minnesota located at the confluence of the Straight and Cannon Rivers. Faribault traced its existence back to a trading post established by Alexander Faribault and his Dakota wife in 1826.[122]

Ralph attended Sacred Heart Catholic School up to 8th Grade. The Roman Catholic faith was strong in his family. Indeed, his older sister Leona would become a Nun. At an early age, Ralph received a religious calling. After completing 8th Grade, thirteen-year-old

---

[122] For more about the City of Faribault, visit their website at https://www.ci.faribault.mn.us/

Ralph entered the Minor Seminary at Nazareth Hall Preparatory Seminary to study for the priesthood. Founded in 1923 in St. Paul, Minnesota, Nazareth Hall prepared young men ages fourteen to twenty-one for the priesthood. It closed in 1970 and today is part of the University of Northwestern. Six years later, Ralph graduated from Nazareth Hall in 1940. He had completed both four years of high school and two years of college at Nazareth Hall. Afterwards, he entered the St. Paul Major Seminary.[123]

About a year later, Ralph decided that the priesthood was not for him. He left St. Paul Major Seminary in 1941 but he did not leave the faith. He stayed in St. Paul and went to work for *The Catholic Digest*.

Like so many Americans, the Japanese attack on Pearl Harbor on 7 December 1941 had a transformative effect on Ralph Thibodeau. Soon after the attack, Ralph enlisted in the Navy's V-5 aviation cadet program at Naval Air Station Minneapolis, Minnesota and became a Naval Aviation Cadet. He reported for Active Duty the following September. The process of becoming a naval aviator through the V-5 program involved first learning how to be a member of the U.S. Navy, then pre-flight training, followed by primary flight training and finally advanced flight training. After reporting for Active Duty, Cadet Thibodeau remained in Minnesota. When he started his Primary Flight Training at NAS Minneapolis, Thibodeau had never even been in an airplane before. His first flight was with an instructor named Nabors in a N2S Stearman biplane, known famously as the "Yellow Peril." Nabors

---

[123] University of Northwestern, St. Paul. "Nazareth Hall." Accessed online on 2 October 2020 at https://www.unwsp.edu/about-us/history-heritage/nazareth-hall

taught the nervous cadet how to relax and control his airplane. "Soon I learned that I could make the plane do what I wanted and became a 'hot pilot' able to execute any maneuver fearlessly," he would later write in an unpublished memoir. Thibodeau completed Primary Flight Training in May 1943 and then went to Advanced Flight Training at NAS Corpus Christi, Texas which was soon known as the "University of the Air." Located on the Texas Gulf Coast, NAS Corpus Christi was a massive complex that had only been commissioned in 1941. The naval air station rapidly grew with the construction of numerous outlying auxiliary airfields. Over the course of the war, some 35,000 pilots would be trained here, including future President of the United States George H. W. Bush and the author's great uncle, LT(jg) James A. Nist. While at NAS Corpus Christi, Ralph met Betty Trader at a dance held in an Episcopal Church in Corpus Christi.[124]

Ralph Thibodeau was commissioned as an ensign and received his Naval Aviator wings in August 1943. He then transferred to NAS Opa Locha near Miami, Florida for training as a fighter pilot. After completing training in fighter tactics, ENS Thibodeau went north to Lake Michigan to perform carrier landing qualifications

---

[124] For more about Naval aviation training in World War Two, see Captain Matt Portz, USN (Ret.)'s "Aviation Training and Expansion – Part 1." *Naval Aviation News.* (July-August 1990), pp. 22-27; and "Aviation Training and Expansion – Part 2." *Naval Aviation News.* (September-October 1990), pp. 22-27.; Norman C. Delaney. "Corpus Christi's 'University of the Air.' *Naval History Magazine* (June 2013). Accessed online on 16 November 2018 at https://www.usni.org/magazines/navalhistory/2013-05/corpus-christis-university-air ; Jimmy Nist reported to NAS Corpus Christi in June 1943 and was commissioned the following September. Later assigned to Fighting Squadron Eighty-Four of *USS Bunker Hill* (CV-17), Nist was killed on 4 April 1945 while flying a combat mission over Amami o Shima in the western Pacific Ocean.

aboard *USS Sable.* The Navy had acquired the converted paddle steamer, slapped a flight deck on her and used her to training pilots in carrier landings. Back at NAS Opa Locha, volunteers were being sought to train as Landing Signal Officers. So ENS Thibodeau volunteered and was sent to NAS Jacksonville, Florida for training. While he was there, Betty Trader flew out to Jacksonville. She and Ralph were married in January 1944. He completed his training in March 1943 and was assigned to Carrier Aircraft Support Unit 21 at NAS Norfolk for further assignment to the Atlantic Fleet.

ENS Thibodeau's marriage to Betty proved of great significance to his naval career. Since he was married, he was assigned to the escort carrier *USS Charger* (CVE-30) which was training pilots in the Chesapeake Bay. In his unpublished memoirs, Thibodeau described his first encounter with the escort carrier:

> I reported for duty aboard the *Charger* about the middle of March, my first experience with any vessel bigger than a flat bottom rowboat. She was a floating city, displacing 14,000 tons, with a flight deck 440 feet long and 40 feet wide, and had nine arresting gear wires, and a double barrier cable forward to stop a plane in case its tail hook didn't grab a wire. She required a crew of 1,500 men."[125]

As a Landing Signal Officer, ENS Thibodeau was responsible for guiding aircraft in their attempts to land aboard *Charger.* The LSO worked from a platform located near the stern on the port side of the flight deck. A life-net was strung below the platform in case the LSO had to get out of the way of an errant aircraft quickly. Using

---

[125] This paragraph was included in Ralph Jr.'s biography of his father.

paddles, the LSO would give the incoming pilots commands to guide them safely onto the ship's flight deck. The LSO would tell the pilot whether he was coming in too high, too low, too fast, or too slow. If the pilot was properly lined up for the landing, the LSO would give him the 'Cut' signal to cut his power and land his aircraft. If at anytime the LSO deemed that the approach was unsafe, he would give the pilot the 'Wave-Off' signal which meant abort the landing and go around for another try. The 'Wave Off' was mandatory.

ENS Thibodeau worked closely with the more experienced LSOs aboard *Charger* for two weeks.   When the Chief LSO was confident that he could handle the responsibility, Thibodeau began performing the duties he had been trained for. In time, Thibodeau would be promoted to the position of Chief Landing Signal Officer. By the time he left *Charger* eighteen months later, the ship had performed 15,000 landings, and Thibodeau had been LSO for about 10,000 of them.

Betty found a place to live in the Norfolk area and so was able to be with her husband when *Charger* was in port. Their first child, daughter Carmen, was born in 1944 in Norfolk.

Chapter Seven
ANDREW S. FUTEY, USNR

Andrew Steve Futey was born on 16 January 1918 on a small farm in the coal and steel town of Monessen in southwestern Pennsylvania. His parents – John and Mary Futey (Futej) – were Slovak immigrants who had come to the United States from the Austria-Hungary Empire only a few years before Andrew's birth. He was one of nine children – seven girls and two boys.

Andrew attended the local high school and studied auto mechanics. Not seeing a future in Monessen aside from working in the local coal mines or steel mills, Andrew dropped out of high school in his junior year and began working.

Some time after Andrew left high school, his father John moved east in search of better economic opportunities. With nine children and a wife to support, John Futey needed a larger income than could be had from farming. John initially sought work in New York City but later moved to Perth Amboy, New Jersey. There, he was able to find a job in an oil refinery that enabled him to save money to bring his family east.

The city of Perth Amboy was located in Middlesex County on the Arthur Kill that separated New Jersey and Staten Island, New York. The city dated back to the early 18th Century. After the Civil War, Perth Amboy experienced major industrialization and immigration. In 1940, Perth Amboy was a city of factories and oil refineries.

After working for a time and saving sufficient money, John Futey sent for his wife and family. His older daughters had by now moved out, were working and getting married. His daughter Margie was living in Manhattan. Andrew came east with his mother Mary and youngest sister Irene and joined the Futey patriarch in Perth Amboy. Andrew got a job driving trucks.

By late summer of 1940, the world was deeply involved in its second global war in less than twenty-five years. Nazi Germany had conquered western and central Europe and divided up Poland with the Soviet Union. On the continent of Asia, Imperial Japan was expanding its territory at China's expense. The United States had thus far remained out of war. It was now trying to prepare itself for a war that seemed inevitable.

As part of the efforts to prepare the nation for war, Congress passed the Selective Training and Service Act of 1940. On 16 September 1940, President Franklin D. Roosevelt signed the Act into law. The Selective Service Act required all men who had reached their 21st birthday but not yet reached their 36th birthday to register for military service. Previously, the Federal government had employed mass conscription for military service during the Civil War and World War One, but had never done so in peacetime.

When the Selective Service Act was enacted, Andrew Futey was twenty-two-years-old and thus required by the new law to register with his Local Draft Board. Andrew accordingly registered for Selective Service on 16 October 1940. At the time, he was living with his parents at 768 State Street in Perth Amboy. He was working for Conrad Seibolt Incorporated which was located at 16-18 Richmond Street in New Brunswick. He was described as being five feet eight inches tall, weighing 150 pounds and having brown eyes and brown hair.[126]

By now his sister Margie was living in New York City at East 73rd Street. At some point, Margie introduced him to Emily Lillian Falat. Margie and Emily lived in the same apartment building. Emily was born on November 23, 1918 and raised in Manhattan. Her parents - John and Mary Falat - were Slovaks who had emigrated from the Austria-Hungarian Empire in November 1899. Prior to emigration, John Falat had been drafted into the Imperial Army and served with an artillery regiment. After coming to America, John went to work for the Interboro Rapid Transit Company that operated underground subways and trains in New York City. Emily had two older brothers and three sisters, one of which died at an early age due to a sudden illness. Her mother had died when Emily was still in school. Emily was living with her father. She had taken some art classes at the Pratt Institute and was working in the garment industry.

Andrew and Emily fell in love and were married on 20 November 1942. The couple settled in Perth Amboy. In January 1943, Andrew

---

[126] I obtained a digital copy of Andrew Futey's Draft Card from www.fold3.com

began working at the City Service Oil Company transferring oil between tank cars and tanker ships. Their first son Andrew John was born in October of that year.

In early 1944, Andrew received notification that he was being drafted into the U.S. Army. As the Army did not appeal to Andrew, he immediately enlisted in the U.S. Navy. He was inducted into the Navy and sent to Naval Training Station Sampson for recruit training (Boot Camp).

Apprentice Seaman Futey arrived at NTS Sampson on 26 February 1944. NTS Sampson was a sprawling recruit training center located on the eastern shore of Lake Seneca in New York State's Finger Lakes region. Construction had begun in late May 1942 and completed only 270 days later. The first recruits arrived for training in October 1942 before the base was completed. Apprentice Seaman Futey was one of over 411,000 Navy recruits to complete Boot Camp at NTS Sampson.[127]

At the end of March 1944, Apprentice Seaman Futey completed recruit training. He was transferred to Receiving Station Norfolk, Virginia on 8 April 1944 and assigned the following day to the escort aircraft carrier *USS Charger* (CVE-30). Now a Seaman 2nd Class, Futey was assigned to work in the carrier's engine room due to his background in auto mechanics and fuel oil systems. Soon after, he received an American Red Cross message informing him that his father had passed away in Perth Amboy. On 1 May 1944,

---

[127] For more about NTS Sampson, visit the NTS Sampson Museum website at www.rpadden.com/sampson.htm. During the 1950s, the U.S. Air Force operated the base as a Basic Training center, training over 330,000 recruits. In 1960, the land was sold to the State of New York who now operates it as a state park and marina.

he was promoted to Fireman 2nd Class, a rate that he would hold for most of his time in service. Later that year, his wife Emily and son Andrew joined him in Norfolk and rented an off base apartment. In November of that year, he attended Fleet Firefighting School. Also that year, Futey earned qualifications for operating compressors and standing watch for throttles and purifiers in the engine room.[128]

Working in the engine room was hot, dirty and sometimes dangerous work. Engine problems had plagued the escort carrier early in her career. One particularly hazardous job involved checking, tightening and lubricating fittings in a confined space in the engine room after the engines had been shut down. Due to the fumes and high heat in the space, sailors could only work in there for a few minutes at a time. On one such occasion, Fireman 2nd Class Futey had taken his turn in the space. The sailor that followed him in the rotation became overcome by the heat and fumes. Despite having just emerged from the space, Futey went back inside and rescued the fallen sailor, losing his wedding ring in the process. Recognizing his bravery, Futey's Chief Petty Officer gave him his own wedding ring to replace the one lost in the space. The Chief told him that he longer needed the ring since he was divorced. Futey accepted the ring as his own and when he told Emily the story, the two considered the gift as their forever bond. He wore this ring from then on.

Having been raised a Roman Catholic, Futey became friendly with the ship's Roman Catholic chaplain. Often he would assist the chaplain at Mass as an altar server.

---

[128] These details are from his personnel records.

Chapter Eight
Mishaps

The U.S. Navy defines an aviation mishap as an unplanned aviation event that results in personal injury or property damage. During her four years of training carrier pilots, *Charger* experienced numerous aviation mishaps. Most were minor affairs but some resulted in the aircraft being severely damaged, destroyed or lost altogether to the depths of the Chesapeake Bay.

Watching the planes landing was a popular pastime for *Charger*'s sailors when they weren't on watch or duty. Andrew Futey would later recall watching the planes landing. He witnessed a number of mishaps, including several in which the aircraft went over the side of the ship and into the water. Watching the planes landing could be a hazardous pastime. On several occasions, *Charger* sailors were injured by errant planes who failed to land properly.

From his position as Charger's Landing Signal Officer, LT Ralph Thibodeau was in a prime viewing location for aviation mishaps. In his unpublished memoirs, Ralph Thibodeau recalled the mishaps that he witnessed:

We had our share of crash landings – inexperienced pilots who made mistakes after I gave them the "Cut" signal, and every two weeks or so the ship had to put into Norfolk to unload the wreckage. We also had a few casualties – pilots, disregarding their altimeters, especially at night, and flying into the water, planes crashing into the bridge, losing a wing and cartwheeling into the drink, and an occasional pilot landing in the catwalk beside the deck instead of on the deck, with one night pilot hitting the deck with a belly tank full of gas, and exploding.[129]

LT Thibodeau had his own near miss by an errant aircraft. He was serving as LSO for night landings when an incoming pilot approached the ship some 25 feet below the level of the flight deck. Despite repeated warnings from Thibodeau that he was too low, the pilot continued on his collision course with the ship's stern. Thibodeau finally decided to vacate the LSO platform but forgot to disconnect his radio cable. With no time to lose, Thibodeau went back to the LSO platform and dove into the safety net. The pilot finally realized his potentially fatal mistake and pulled up. His arresting hook nearly caught the bar which supported the safety net that Thibodeau was seeking refuge in.[130]

---

[129] Quoted in Ralph A. Thibodeau Jr.'s biography of his father.

[130] From Ralph A. Thibodeau Jr.'s August 2020 biography of his father.

Chapter Nine
USS Charger in 1944

Andrew Futey joined the Navy at a time when the tides of war had turned against the Axis Powers in both the European / Atlantic and Pacific Theaters. Allied forces were preparing for the invasion of Normandy scheduled for June 1944. The Central Pacific drive had taken the Marshall Islands and the Gilbert Islands and had set its sights on the Marianas Islands. There continued to be a great need for qualified naval aviators and *USS Charger* was at the forefront of the Navy's efforts to qualify its aviators for carrier service.

Charger did not have any aircraft permanently assigned to her except for two or three amphibious planes. She had a Shore Based Detachment which worked out of Hangar LP-3 at East Field, Naval Air Station Norfolk. She also worked in conjunction with Carrier Air Support Unit 21 (CASU-21). In March 1944, *Charger* started working with squadrons based as Oceana Field.[131]

Throughout 1944 and 1945, carrier landing qualifications were fast paced aboard *Charger.* Those squadrons needing to qualify their pilots for carrier service would first received an indoctrination

---

[131] U.S. Navy. *USS Charger.* CVE-30 History of *USS Charger* (CVE-30). 24 May 1945. RG38. NARA. Archives II. [Hereafter cited as *Charger* History.]

session by *Charger*'s Shore Based Detachment officers. After indoctrination, the squadron aircraft would rendezvous with *Charger* operating out in the Chesapeake Bay. On most days, multiple squadrons would cycle through *Charger*.[132]

Charger went into the Norfolk Navy Yard at the end of December 1943 for maintenance and stayed there until 6 January 1944. Her maintenance period completed, *Charger* was ordered to the operating area to conduct flight operations. She performed flight operations for most of January, returning to Hampton Roads on 22 January.[133]

Charger conducted flight operations on fourteen days in the month of February 1944. The squadrons that trained aboard *Charger* during February were Fighting Thirteen, Torpedo Thirteen, Bombing Thirteen and Composite Squadrons Six and Ninety-Five. 923 landings were performed aboard ship with only three aviation mishaps that month. There were two barrier crashes and one aircraft crashed into the port catwalk. The most serious mishap occurred on 7 February. A VF-13 Hellcat crashed into the upper section of the crash barrier and came to rest on the forward end of the flight deck. The Hellcat came to rest in such a way that the ship's salvage crew could not remove the aircraft without inflicting serious additional damage to it. This forced *Charger* to suspend flight operations and return to Norfolk. At Norfolk, yard cranes removed the Hellcat which surprisingly had sustained only slight

---

[132] U.S. Navy. *USS Charger.* CVE-30 History of *USS Charger* (CVE-30). 24 May 1945. RG38. NARA. Archives II. [Hereafter cited as *Charger* History.]

[133] U.S. Navy. Atlantic Fleet. Fleet Air Command, Norfolk. War Diary. January 1944. RG38, NARA. Archives II.

damage. From 14 February to 20 February, *Charger* was at Imperial Docks, Berkley, Virginia for engine maintenance. The starboard engine was overhauled and the port engine was inspected. On 21 February, RADM A. C. Read came aboard to observe flight operations.[134]

Charger conducted flight operations on sixteen of thirty-one days in March 1944. Eight U.S. Navy and three Royal Navy squadrons trained aboard the escort carrier that month. The number of landings that month (915) was just slightly below the previous month's total. There were eight mishaps, two of which involved severe damage to the aircraft involved. On the first of the month, Charger performed sixty-four landings. Of these, thirty-seven landings were done by SB2C Helldivers with a new experimental propeller. To maintain their combat proficiency, Charger's crew performed short range battle practice on 14 March and 22 March using the ship's 3-inch/.50 caliber and 5-inch/.51 caliber guns and anti-aircraft gun practice using 20mm Oerlikon anti-aircraft cannons on 24 March. Then on 28 March, Charger transferred 140 trained sailors to serve with fleet units.[135]

During April 1944, *Charger* performed 1,883 landings and qualified 362 pilots. *Charger* also experienced sixteen aviation mishaps. Most of the mishaps were minor crashes with minor

---

[134] U.S. Navy. USS Charger. CVE-30. War Diary 1 FEB 1944 to 29 FEB 1944. 10 March 1944. RG38, NARA, Archives II.

[135] U.S. Navy. USS Charger. CVE-30. War Diary. 1 March to 31 March 1944. 3 April 1944. RG38, NARA, Archives II.

injuries and slight damage to the aircraft involved. Nevertheless, these mishaps added up.[136]

One of the squadrons that trained aboard *Charger* in April 1944 was Fighting Squadron Eighty (VF-80). VF-80 had been commissioned at Naval Air Station Atlantic City, New Jersey on 1 February 1944. On 1 April 1944, VF-80 re-located to Naval Auxiliary Air Station (NAAS) Oceana, Virginia. There the squadron joined Bombing Squadron Eighty and Torpedo Squadron Eighty to form Air Group Eighty. VF-80 was equipped with thirty-six F6F Hellcat fighters.[137]

From 3 April to 6 April, *Charger* hosted four squadrons which performed 464 landings aboard her. 106 of these landings were performed at night. Forty-eight pilots were qualified in carrier landings. There were also two major mishaps. On 5 April, a TBM Avenger crashed through the barriers and into two other Avengers which were spotted on the forward flight deck. Two Avengers were seriously damaged and one suffered minor damage. The next day, a SB2C-1C Helldiver suffered a serious crash. "Because the hangar deck space was filled with damaged planes, proceeded from

---

[136] U.S. Navy. *USS Charger.* CVE-30 War Diary for April 1944. 1 May 1944. RG38, NARA, Archives II.

[137] U.S. Navy. Fighting Squadron Eighty. History of Fighting Squadron Eighty. 6 September 1944. RG38, NARA, Archives II. After carrier qualifications, VF-80 and Air Group 80 embarked aboard *USS Ticonderoga* (CV-14) in June 1944. Both would later participate in the liberation of the Philippines, and air raids on Formosa, French Indochina, and Iwo Jima.

the operating area to Hampton Roads, Va., and discharged the damaged planes," reported the ship's War Diary.[138]

After offloading the damaged aircraft, *Charger* went immediately back to the operating area and resumed flight operations. On 7 April and 8 April, 270 landings were performed by Bombing Squadron Eighty and Royal Navy Squadron No. 738. There was only one mishap: a SNJ crashed into the barrier.[139]

On 8 April, *Charger* made a brief return to the Hampton Roads anchorage. The following day, she received one hundred new enlisted sailors who had recently completely completed Recruit Training. Among this group was Seaman 2nd Class Andrew S. Futey. Originally from Monessen, Pennsylvania, Futey had moved to Perth Amboy, New Jersey and married the former Emily Falat the preceding November. Futey was assigned to work in the engine rooms.

Charger's stay at the Hampton Roads anchorage was brief. On 10 April, she was back in the operating area conducting flight operations. VC-15, VC-19 and VF-80 performed carrier landing qualifications. One TBF Avenger and one F6F Hellcat had minor crashes with minimal damage on 11 April. On 13 April, two VF-80 Hellcats had barrier crashes and another Hellcat crashed into the port catwalk. The pilot was slightly injured. Once again, *Charger*'s hangar deck was filled with damaged aircraft, and so the ship departed the operating area. This time she went back to Naval

---

[138] U.S. Navy. *USS Charger.* CVE-30 War Diary for April 1944. 1 May 1944. RG38, NARA, Archives II.

[139] U.S. Navy. *USS Charger.* CVE-30 War Diary for April 1944. 1 May 1944. RG38, NARA, Archives II.

Operating Base Norfolk where she refueled, took on provisions and offloaded damaged aircraft.[140]

On 17 April, *Charger* again went north to the operating area for flight operations. On that day, VC-55 pilots performed a total of 174 landings. There were no flight operations for the next two days due to low wind velocity. The winds were sufficient on 20 April for flight operations. Bombing Squadron Eighty performed 79 landings and had two minor crashes. *Charger* then conducted flight operations for the next eight days. VT-301, Royal Navy Squadron No. 856, VT-13, VF-80, VC-80, VC-69, and VC-6 performed carrier qualifications during this time. On 23 April, a Hellcat and a Helldiver each had minor mishaps during landings. The following day, another Hellcat had a minor mishap. On 26 April, a FM-2 Wildcat lost power while taking off, and crashed into the water. The pilot was rescued but the plane was lost. On 27 April, a TBM Avenger from VC-69 crashed into the barrier and another Avenger from VC-6 crashed into the port catwalk.[141]

April 1944 had been a very busy month for *USS Charger* with sixteen aviation mishaps. Two Avengers were seriously damaged and one Wildcat was lost in the waters of the Chesapeake Bay. Fortunately, there were no serious injuries to any pilots or ship's crew.[142]

---

[140] U.S. Navy. *USS Charger.* CVE-30 War Diary for April 1944. 1 May 1944. RG38, NARA, Archives II.

[141] U.S. Navy. *USS Charger.* CVE-30 War Diary for April 1944. 1 May 1944. RG38, NARA, Archives II.

[142] U.S. Navy. *USS Charger.* CVE-30 War Diary for April 1944. 1 May 1944. RG38, NARA, Archives II.

In the month of May 1944, *Charger* had a little more than half the number of landings of the previous month but only four less aviation mishaps. Eleven squadrons conducted training including two from the British Royal Navy.[143]

Charger began the month by hosting a group of civilian dignitaries. Management and labor leaders from the petroleum industry and media reporters came aboard to observe flight operations on 1 May. This included carrier landings and a simulated aerial attack upon the ship. The following day, pilots from Composite Squadrons Six and Sixty-Nine and Observation Fighter Squadron Two performed a total of forty-seven landings aboard *Charger.* Afterwards, *Charger* returned to NOB Norfolk for several days of refueling, maintenance and upkeep.[144]

Charger was back in the operating area on 7 May. The next ten days were high tempo with flight operations on eight of those days and battle training on the other two days. This cycle of training started inauspiciously. Composite Squadrons Eight and Twelve performed 151 landings but had two serious crashes aboard the carrier. Though there were no injuries to pilot or ship's crew, both aircraft were heavily damaged. The following day, the carrier hosted Night Fighting Squadron Seventy-Nine. VFN-79 performed sixty landings during the day and another sixty-six at night. Composite Squadron Eight performed 104 landings on 9 May and qualified twenty-two of its pilots with no mishaps. Only two landings occurred on 10 May due to low wind velocity. There

---

[143] U.S. Navy. *USS Charger.* CVE-30 War Diary for May 1944. 1 June 1944. RG38, NARA, Archives II.

[144] U.S. Navy. *USS Charger.* CVE-30 War Diary for May 1944. 1 June 1944. RG38, NARA, Archives II.

were forty-three landings on 11 May as Night Fighting Squadron Seventy-Eight and Observation - Fighting Squadron Two performed carrier qualifications. There were 106 day landings and 33 night landings aboard *Charger* on 12 May with two aircraft crashing into the ship's catwalks. On 13 May, Navy Bombing Squadron Eighty and Royal Navy Squadron No. 841 performed a total of 108 landings. They also experienced one deck crash and two barrier crashes. Two of the aircraft suffered minor damage while one aircraft was severely damaged. The next day, Royal Navy Squadron No. 1841 performed only seven landings but had one barrier crash. *Charger* conducted local battle area practice on 15 May, including live firing of its 3-inch, 5-inch and 20mm weapons. Another fifty landings were completed on 16 May and *Charger* returned to NOB Norfolk later that day.[145]

Charger remained at NOB Norfolk for the next week. On 22 May, the carrier returned to the operating area for carrier qualifications. Sixty-nine landings were done on that day. A VB-80 Helldiver crashed into the top of the barrier and went over the bow into the water. The pilot was rescued but the aircraft was lost. *Charger* conducted carrier qualifications until 29 May. During this time, there were three serious aviation mishaps. On 27 May, a Helldiver missed the arresting wires and crashed into the island and the barrier. The aircraft caught fire and was severely damaged. Fortunately there were no injuries. Later that day, another Helldiver was waved off from its landing attempt. The Helldiver then unexpectedly lost power and crashed into the water. The pilot was rescued but the aircraft was lost. Two days later a TBM

---

[145] U.S. Navy. *USS Charger.* CVE-30 War Diary for May 1944. 1 June 1944. RG38, NARA, Archives II.

Avenger crashed into the barrier and *Charger*'s island. The aircraft was badly damaged but there were no injuries.[146]

Thus ended May 1944. It was another month of mangled aircraft. Altogether for the month, there were twelve crashes or mishaps. Of these, two aircraft were lost into the Chesapeake Bay, one was seriously damaged by fire, and four other aircraft sustained major damage.[147]

June 1944 was one of the most significant months of World War Two for the Western Allies. On 4 June, Allied forces liberated Rome, the Eternal City. Two days later, British, Canadian and American forces landed on the Normandy coast to begin the liberation of western Europe. On 15 June, U.S. Marines and soldiers landed on Saipan Island of the Marianas Islands in an invasion almost as large as the D-Day invasion two weeks before. Four days later, the American and Japanese carrier forces clashed in the climactic Battle of the Philippine Sea which devastated the latter's carriers and carrier air forces.

Meanwhile in the Chesapeake Bay, *USS Charger* was busy training carrier pilots for war. Charger conducted flight operations from 4 June to 7 June. During this time, 265 landings were performed by pilots assigned to five U.S. Navy squadrons and one Royal Navy squadron. There was only one mishap. An aircraft attempting a

---

[146] U.S. Navy. *USS Charger.* CVE-30 War Diary for May 1944. 1 June 1944. RG38, NARA, Archives II.

[147] U.S. Navy. *USS Charger.* CVE-30 War Diary for May 1944. 1 June 1944. RG38, NARA, Archives II.

night landing on 6 June crashed over the starboard bow and into the water. The pilot was rescued but the plane was lost.[148]

On the morning of 20 June 1944, *Charger* weighed anchor and headed to its operating area. Over the next six days, *Charger* conducted a busy schedule of flight operations. A total of 522 landings were performed on her decks and 64 pilots from eight different squadrons were qualified. But those six days in late June 1944 were also a dangerous time with a total of ten serious mishaps occurring. One sailor was killed and three were injured. Three aircraft were lost and seven aircraft were slightly damaged.[149]

That first day of carrier operations, 20 June 1944, proved to be a deadly day. On this day, pilots from Bombing Squadron VB-82 and Fighting Squadron VF-82 were performing their landing qualifications. A total of 119 landings were performed and 18 pilots from the two squadrons were qualified. However, one attempted landing ended in tragedy. The aircraft crashed into the starboard catwalk and then went over the side into the water. The plane was lost and the pilot escaped with only minor injuries. Two *Charger* sailors were not so fortunate. While on the catwalk, they were struck by the errant aircraft. One sailor was killed and the other suffered multiple injuries.[150]

---

[148] U.S. Navy. *USS Charger.* CVE-30 War Diary for June 1944. 3 July 1944. RG, 38, NARA, Archives II.

[149] U.S. Navy. *USS Charger.* CVE-30 War Diary for June 1944. 3 July 1944. RG, 38, NARA, Archives II.

[150] U.S. Navy. *USS Charger.* CVE-30 War Diary for June 1944. 3 July 1944. RG, 38, NARA, Archives II. See Entry for 20 June 1944.

The following day, Composite Squadrons Twelve and Thirteen and Bombing Squadron Eighty-Two completed 126 successful landings aboard *Charger*. There were also two crashes. One aircraft crashed into the starboard catwalk; fortunately there were no injuries and only minor damage to the aircraft. Another plane went over the starboard bow and into the water. The plane was lost but the pilot was rescued.[151]

On 22 June, Fighting Squadron Eighty-Two and Torpedo Squadron Eighty-Two performed sixty-nine landings. There were also three crashes but no injuries. The next day there were just twenty-six landings. On 24 June, Royal Navy Squadrons No. 1820 and No. 1843, and U.S. Navy squadron VCS-8 performed 134 landings. One aircraft crashed into the barrier and another one went over the starboard bow into the water. The plane was lost but the pilot was rescued. Two more crashes occurred on 25 June and 162 successful landings. After a couple days off, *Charger* finished the month with 238 successful landings and no crashes or mishaps.[152]

In addition to their initial carrier training aboard *Charger*, pilots routinely sought their carrier qualifications requisite for deploying aboard the Navy's combat carriers. Carrier Air Group 82, consisting of Fighting Squadron 82 (VF-82), Bombing Squadron 82 (VB-82) and Torpedo Squadron 82 (VT-82), earned their carrier qualifications aboard *Charger*. In late 1944, the air group embarked on *USS Bennington* (CV-20). In February 1945, they participated in the Navy's first carrier air strikes against the

---

[151] U.S. Navy. *USS Charger*. CVE-30 War Diary for June 1944. 3 July 1944. RG, 38, NARA, Archives II. See Entry for 21 June 1944.

[152] U.S. Navy. *USS Charger*. CVE-30 War Diary for June 1944. 3 July 1944. RG, 38, NARA, Archives II.

Japanese Home Islands. The pilots and aircrew of these squadrons would conduct missions from *Bennington* until June 1945.[153]

Compared with prior months, *Charger* conducted much fewer carrier qualifications in July 1944. Nevertheless the month was significant for several important reasons. In the first two weeks of the month, *Charger* conducted flight operations on eight days. There were 809 landings aboard the ship, including three straight days of 200+ landings. There were three barrier crashes, one of which resulted in major damage to the aircraft. On 9 July, another aircraft was heavily damaged when it crashed into *Charger*'s island. The next day, *Charger* returned to the Hampton Roads anchorage. An inspection team from the Bureau of Aeronautics came aboard to examine the Number One arresting gear which had been experiencing serious problems. On 11 July, *Charger* was back in the operating area. Fighting Squadron 82 performed forty-three carrier landings. Two days later, *Charger* hosted a group of civilians from the aircraft manufacturing industry and labor unions. Thirteen carrier landings were performed by six different aircraft types as well as a demonstration of catapult launches and a simulated air attack upon the ship. In addition, Commander, Naval Air Forces Atlantic (COMNAVAIRLANT) VADM Patrick Nieson Lynch Bellinger, USN, landed an aircraft aboard the ship.[154]

VADM Bellinger had a long and distinguished naval career that dated back to the US Naval Academy Class of 1907. A month after

---

[153] Samuel Eliot Morison. *History of United States Naval Operations in World War II. Volume XIV - Victory in the Pacific.* (Boston: Little, Brown & Co., 1960.) Appendix 1 details the composition of the carrier forces involved in the last campaigns in the Pacific Theater.

[154] U.S. Navy. *USS Charger.* CVE-30 War Diary for July 1944. 8 August 1944. RG, 38, NARA, Archives II.

graduating from Annapolis, Bellinger joined the crew of the battleship *USS Vermont* and participated in the Great White Fleet's cruise around the world. He began his service with naval aviation in November 1912 at the Naval Academy. From December 1917 to March 1919, he served as the first commanding officer of Naval Air Station Hampton Roads (later renamed NAS Norfolk). His other noteworthy accomplishments included commanding the seaplane *NC-1* for its historic trans-Atlantic flight from Newfoundland to the Azones in 1919, commanding the aircraft carrier *USS Ranger* (CV-4) from June 1936 to June 1937, serving as Commander Patrol Wings, Pacific Fleet from May to August 1942, and serving as Deputy Chief of Staff to the Commander-in-Chief, U.S. Fleet from August 1942 to March 1943. He was also Commander of Patrol Wing Two and Commander, Aircraft, Scouting Force during the Pearl Harbor attack. He directed that the famed message "Air raid, Pearl Harbor. This is no drill" be sent out.[155]

After hosting its distinguished guests, *Charger* put into Naval Operating Base Norfolk and tied up to Pier #5 on 14 July. For the next three days, *Charger*'s troublesome Number One arresting

---

[155] Ira R. Hanna, "One Century Ago: Naval Air Station Norfolk's First Skipper, Part 1:   P.N.L. Bellinger: Pioneer Naval Aviator and the Early Days of NAS Norfolk." Hampton Roads Naval Museum Blog. August 27, 2018. Accessed online on 9 June 2020 at https://hamptonroadsnavalmuseum.blogspot.com/search?q=bellinger ; Ira R. Hanna, "One Century Ago: Naval Air Station Norfolk's First Skipper, Part 2." Hampton Roads Naval Museum Blog. September 21, 2018. Accessed online on 9 June 2020 at https://hamptonroadsnavalmuseum.blogspot.com/2018/09/one-century-ago-naval-air-station.html ; Naval History and Heritage Command. "Patrick Nieson Lynch Bellinger   8 October 1885 - 29 May 1962." Accessed on 9 June 2020 at https://www.history.navy.mil/research/library/research-guides/modern-biographical-files-ndl/modern-bios-b/bellinger-patrick-n.html

equipment was re-aligned and re-conditioned. Two more days of flight operations followed with a total of 216 landings performed by Fighting Squadron Eighty-Two and Torpedo Squadron Eighty-Two. Two aircraft had minor crashes into the port catwalk.[156]

On 21 July, *Charger* put in at Norfolk Navy Yard for its annual overhaul. The overhaul occupied the next three weeks. Coming out of the Navy Yard on 15 August, *Charger* then performed three days of post repair trials.[157]

Having completed its post-repair trials, *Charger* conducted flight operations on ten of the remaining thirteen days in August. On 22 August, representatives of the Glenn L. Martin Aircraft Company observed flight operations by Bombing Squadron Eighty-Six and Fighting Squadron Eighty-Two. Eight squadrons performed 702 day and night landings aboard *Charger* during the second half of August. There were seven aviation mishaps. On 21 August, two F6F-5 Hellcats crashed into the barriers. The following day, a SB2C from Bombing Eighty-Six crashed on the forward end of the flight deck. While attempting a landing, a VF-82 Hellcat caught an arresting wire but the wire parted. The Hellcat then crashed into the barrier with minor damage to the aircraft. Unfortunately, the parting arresting wire struck a *Charger* enlisted sailor, injuring his back. On 24 August, a F4U Corsair of Royal Navy Squadron No. 1846 crashed over the port side. The pilot was rescued but the plane was lost. The next day, another of the squadron's Corsairs

---

156 U.S. Navy. *USS Charger.* CVE-30 War Diary for July 1944. 8 August 1944. RG, 38, NARA, Archives II.

157 U.S. Navy. *USS Charger.* CVE-30 War Diary for July 1944. 8 August 1944. RG, 38, NARA, Archives II.; U.S. Navy. *USS Charger.* CVE-30 War Diary for August 1944. 1 September 1944. RG, 38, NARA, Archives II.

struck *Charger*'s pilot house with its starboard wing. The final mishap of August occurred when an aircraft from Composite Squadron Eight missed the arresting wires and crashed into the barrier. The aircraft sustained major damage.[158]

On 26 August 1944, CAPT Ralph W. D. Woods was relieved by CAPT Robert Ruffin Johnson. During Woods time in command, approximately 12,000 carrier landings were performed aboard *Charger.* Born in Detroit, Michigan on 15 July 1902, CAPT Johnson was a 1926 graduate of the U.S. Naval Academy. In June 1942, he flew a SBD Dauntless dive-bomber off the carrier *USS Hornet* (CV-8) during the Battle of Midway.[159]

Bombing Squadron Eighty-Six performed landings aboard *Charger* in August and September 1944. There was one mishap in August and two in September. On 22 August, LT J. T. Lake crashed his Helldiver into the barrier. On 16 September ENS D. E. Prince experienced a tail hook bounce while attempting to land and crashed into the barrier. His Helldiver suffered significant damage. The propellor was damaged beyond repair, the engine cowling was pierced by the propellor, six inches of the right wing tip buckled, and the wheel fairings were bent. The next day, LT(jg) R. B. Ward landed his Helldiver off center to the right with his left wing low. The aircraft caught the number #2 wire, and skidded onto the port

---

[158] U.S. Navy. *USS Charger.* CVE-30 War Diary for August 1944. 1 September 1944. RG, 38, NARA, Archives II.

[159] U.S. Navy. *USS Charger.* CVE-30 History of *USS Charger* (CVE-30). 24 May 1945. RG38. NARA. Archives II. [Hereafter cited as *Charger* History.]; The biographical information on CAPT Johnson is from www.findagrave.com

catwalk. The propellor blades of Ward's Helldiver were sheared and bent. Its flaps were damaged flaps. The underside of the Helldiver's fuselage was buckled and bent.[160]

The pace of flight operations increased dramatically increased in the month of September 1944. Though only eight squadrons trained with *Charger,* they completed 1,733 successful landings. Flight operations were performed on sixteen of thirty days that month, including six nights of carrier qualifications. On 22 September, there were 83 day landings and 32 night landings.[161]

With increased flight operations, there were also more aviation mishaps, including several serious ones. On the first day of September, an aircraft caught the Number 8 arresting wire but still crashed into *Charger*'s island. Six days later, *Charger* had two crashes on deck, one of which badly damaged the aircraft. The next day, an aircraft crashed into the port catwalk. The day after that, there were three crashes. On 10 September, there were two crashes. One aircraft went into the barrier. Another aircraft struck the ship's Captain's Gig and the port gangway, then went over the port side and into the water. The plane was lost. The pilot was recovered. Both the Captain's Gig and the port gangway were damaged. ENS D. E. Prince's Helldiver from VB-86 crashed into the barrier on 16 September. Another VB-86 aircraft crashed into

---

[160] U.S. Navy. Bombing Squadron Eighty-Six. War Diary September 1944. 30 September 1944. RG38, NARA, Archives II.; U.S. Navy. Bombing Squadron Eighty-Six. War History. Part III Appendix 4 – Accident Summary. RG38, NARA, Archives II.

[161] U.S. Navy. *USS Charger.* CVE-30 War Diary for September 1944. 1 October 1944. RG38, NARA, Archives II.

the port catwalk on 17 September, and there were barrier crashes on 23 and 24 September. Also on 24 September, an aircraft missed the arresting wires, crashed over the forward edge of the flight deck and ended up on the forecastle. The plane's tail section was salvaged and the rest was jettisoned overboard.[162]

On 26 September, *Charger* hosted a group of representatives of the aircraft manufacturing industry and several newspaper reporters for the standard demonstration of carrier operations and simulated air attacks. Six different aircraft types performed fifteen landings and two catapult launches.[163]

October 1944 was a very busy month...even by *Charger*'s vigorous flight schedule. On 4 October, a team from *USS Tulagi* (CVE-72) conducted *Charger*'s annual military inspection. Torpedo defense and gunnery exercises were performed. In twenty days of flight operations, there were 3,038 landings aboard *Charger* or an average of 152 per day. On six of those days, there were over 200 landings aboard the carrier.[164]

There were also fifteen mishaps in the month of October 1944, including two with injuries to the pilots, three aircraft lost in the water, one aircraft wrecked on the flight deck, and one pilot fatality. On 2 October, a F6F Hellcat of Navy Fighting Squadron

---

[162] U.S. Navy. *USS Charger.* CVE-30 War Diary for September 1944. 1 October 1944. RG38, NARA, Archives II.

[163] U.S. Navy. *USS Charger.* CVE-30 War Diary for September 1944. 1 October 1944. RG38, NARA, Archives II.

[164] U.S. Navy. *USS Charger.* CVE-30 War Diary for October 1944. 1 November 1944. RG38, NARA, Archives II.

87 crashed into *Charger*'s island. The pilot suffered only minor injuries but his plane was wrecked. On 7 October, one aircraft brushed the island with its wing while landing and another tipped over while taking off and struck its propeller on the flight deck. The following day, an aircraft caught an arresting wire but its tail hook pulled out and the aircraft crashed into the barrier. There was another barrier crash on 10 October. In an unrelated incident, the Flight Deck Officer ENS C. E. Cassaway suffered a broken left foot when he was struck by an arresting wire. There were two more barrier crashes on 14 October, one barrier crash on 22 October, and two barrier crashes on 26 October. On 16 October, the tail hook of a landing aircraft got caught on the elevator deck edge plate and was torn from its aircraft. The aircraft then crashed into the barrier. The next day, ENS Alfred Michele DeCasro of VB-15 crashed his Helldiver while landing aboard the ship. On 29 October, an aircraft preparing to take-off failed to release its brakes and nosed over. Its propeller struck the flight deck and suffered minor damage.[165]

Three aircraft were lost in the month of October. On 15 October, an aircraft took off from *Charger* but then crashed into the water off the port bow. Later that same day, an aircraft attempting to

---

[165] U.S. Navy. *USS Charger.* CVE-30 War Diary for October 1944. 1 November 1944. RG38, NARA, Archives II.; U.S. Navy. Fighting Squadron Eighty-Seven. War Diary for October 1944. 4 November 1944. RG38, NARA, Archives II.; U.S. Navy. Pacific Fleet. Air Forces, Pacific Fleet. Fighting Squadron Eighty-Seven. War History. 20 October 1945. RG38, NARA, Archives II.; U.S. Navy. Bombing Squadron Fifteen. War History. RG38, NARA, Archives II. ENS DeCasro crashed a Helldiver into *USS Hornet*'s after five-inch gun mount on 7 January 1945 after his arresting hook bounced while attempting to land.

land caught an arresting wire but careened into the port catwalk and went over the side into the water. Both planes were lost but both pilots were rescued. Tragedy struck on 27 October. While attempting to land, a VF-87 Hellcat piloted by ENS Leon J. Lauriun struck the after end of the flight deck, and crashed over the port catwalk and into the water. The plane was lost and the pilot was killed.[166]

Sunday 15 October 1944 was an extraordinary day in the history of *USS Charger.* Not only did the carrier perform its 31,000th landing but it also conducted a record 404 day landings. A unique set of circumstances enabled this tremendous feat to be accomplished. Being Sunday there wasn't any firing practice anywhere in the bay. In addition, there was a 27 to 29 knot headwind. "This enabled the ship to make a longer northerly run and not once during the day did the *Charger* have a down wind run," explained the ship's history. "There was perfect teamwork on the part of the ship's personnel, pilots, and Shore Detachment. Rendezvous was made on time and intervals in the landing circle were so timed that often the ship was averaging a landing per minute." That night the crew enjoyed a movie in the hangar deck

---

[166] U.S. Navy. *USS Charger.* CVE-30 War Diary for October 1944. 1 November 1944. RG38, NARA, Archives II.; U.S. Navy. Fighting Squadron Eighty-Seven. War Diary for October 1944. 4 November 1944. RG38, NARA, Archives II.; U.S. Navy. Pacific Fleet. Air Forces, Pacific Fleet. Fighting Squadron Eighty-Seven. War History. 20 October 1945. RG38, NARA, Archives II.

and CAPT Johnson congratulated his crew for their accomplishment.[167]

Navy Fighting Squadron 87 was one of the squadrons that performed carrier qualifications aboard *USS Charger* in October 1944. The squadron was based at NAAS Oceana to the southeast of Norfolk. They had begun to receive new F6F-5 Hellcats, but instead chose to qualify with its older F6F-3 Hellcats. Their training was interrupted towards the end of the month due to a hurricane which was threatening the Virginia coast. On 19 October, VF-87 flew its aircraft south to North Carolina to get them out of the way of the hurricane. After the storm passed without incident, VF-87 returned to NAAS Oceana.[168]

Unfortunately, October 1944 was not kind to VF-87. The squadron had five major accidents in the month of October 1944. They lost three aircraft into the Chesapeake Bay, one aircraft destroyed aboard *Charger* and a fifth aircraft seriously damaged. The first mishap occurred when ENS Alfred Lerch crashed his Hellcat into *Charger*'s island on 2 October. Lerch suffered only minor injuries but his plane was wrecked. On 10 October, ENS W. V. Hemphill had a hard wheels first landing that required major repairs to his

---

[167] U.S. Navy. *USS Charger.* CVE-30 History of *USS Charger* (CVE-30). 24 May 1945. RG38. NARA. Archives II. [Hereafter cited as *Charger* History.]; U.S. Navy. *USS Charger.* CVE-30 War Diary for October 1944. 1 November 1944. RG38, NARA, Archives II.

[168] U.S. Navy. Fighting Squadron Eighty-Seven. War Diary for October 1944. 4 November 1944. RG38, NARA, Archives II.; U.S. Navy. Pacific Fleet. Air Forces, Pacific Fleet. Fighting Squadron Eighty-Seven. War History. 20 October 1945. RG38, NARA, Archives II.

aircraft. On 15 October, the squadron lost two of its aircraft over the side of *Charger.* Both pilots – Ensigns Emmet W. Payne and George F. Bonifoent were rescued.[169]

The fifth and final accident of October occurred on 27 October. While attempting to land on *Charger*, ENS Leon J. Lauriun struck the end of the flight deck, demolishing his Hellcat. The wreckage tumbled into the water with Lauriun still inside.   Despite an extensive search, Lauriun was not found. He remains to this day as officially listed as Missing in Action. He is memorialized on the East Coast Memorial in New York among the missing from World War Two's Battle of the Atlantic.   October 1944 was a very bad month for Fighting Squadron Eighty-Seven.[170]

---

[169] U.S. Navy. Fighting Squadron Eighty-Seven. War Diary for October 1944. 4 November 1944. RG38, NARA, Archives II.; U.S. Navy. Pacific Fleet. Air Forces, Pacific Fleet. Fighting Squadron Eighty-Seven. War History. 20 October 1945. RG38, NARA, Archives II.

[170] U.S. Navy. Fighting Squadron Eighty-Seven. War Diary for October 1944. 4 November 1944. RG38, NARA, Archives II.; U.S. Navy. Pacific Fleet. Air Forces, Pacific Fleet. Fighting Squadron Eighty-Seven. War History. 20 October 1945. RG38, NARA, Archives II.; VF-87 continued to be plagued with troubles in November. On 9 November ENS Ralph Wetzel failed to pull out of a dive while conducting rocket training and was killed. Periodically, the squadron was called upon to provide pilots for Navy Bombing Fighting Squadron Eighty-Seven which was in the process of formation. Though embarked aboard *USS Randolph* (CV-15) in November, VF-87 and Air Group 87 were deemed not combat ready in January and so transferred off *Randolph*. In May 1945, the Air Group got its chance to prove itself in combat when it was embarked aboard *USS Ticonderoga* (CV-14). VF-87 and Air Group 87 participated in the final aerial operations of the war in the Pacific and were present in Tokyo Bay for the Japanese surrender in September 1945. Afterwards, VF-87 flew reconnaissance missions to locate and provide supplies for Allied Prisoner of War camps locate in the Japanese Home Islands.

Also qualifying in the month of October 1944 aboard *USS Charger* was Bombing Squadron Eighty-Seven. During its flight operations aboard *Charger*, VB-87 had one of the most unusual experiences for either the ship or the squadron. LT Henry Minot was piloting a SB2C Helldiver for a night take-off from the carrier. After launching from *Charger*, LT Minot discovered that he had two passengers in his aircraft when should not have had any passengers. Apparently while Minot's Helldiver was preparing for take off, LT Kanaga of VB-87 had climbed into the rear seat of the Helldiver unbeknownst to Minot. The plane captain was assisting LT Kanaga in strapping in when the Flight Deck Officer signaled Minot to take off. Kanaga quickly pulled the plane captain into the aircraft head first. LT Minot got airborne only to discover LT Kanaga and the Plane Captain in the rear seat of his Helldiver. Rather than return to *Charger* for a night landing, LT Minot flew his Helldiver with its two extra persons on to NAAS Oceana as originally planned.[171]

On 21 November, a group of thirty-nine visitors witnessed a mock air attack while aboard *Charger*. 1,176 landings were performed aboard *Charger* during November 1944 by eight U.S. Navy squadrons and one Royal Navy squadron. There were thirteen mishaps. Two planes were lost in the waters of the Chesapeake Bay and another was destroyed on the flight deck due to a landing mishap. On 23 November, an aircraft attempting to land was waved off its final approach. The aircraft immediately spun in and crashed into the water. The pilot was rescued but the aircraft joined so many others on the bottom of the bay. On 15 November,

---

[171] U.S. Navy. Bombing Squadron Eighty-Seven. War Diary for October 1944. 4 November 1944. RG38, NARA, Archives II.; U.S. Navy. Bombing Squadron Eighty-Seven. History of Bombing Squadron Eighty-Seven. Undated. RG38, NARA, Archives II.

an aircraft missed the wires, crashed through the barrier and went over the port bow into the water. The pilot was rescued; the aircraft was not. On 9 November, an aircraft on the hangar deck caught fire. Fortunately, the fire was quickly extinguished without any injuries or damage to the aircraft. The most serious mishap of the month occurred on 2 November. While attempting to land, an aircraft crashed into the starboard catwalk and stack. It burst into flames. *Charger*'s crew sprang into action, but the aircraft was destroyed and the pilot seriously burned.[172]

While she lay at anchor in Hampton Roads on 27 November 1944, *Charger* was struck by a barge that was being towed. The barge tore a large hole in the bow about fifteen feet above the waterline. *Charger* then proceeded to Naval Base Norfolk for repairs.[173]

Bombing Squadron Sixteen had a rough month in December 1944 with eight aviation mishaps and two aircraft damaged beyond repair. Seven of the squadron's mishaps occurred aboard *USS Charger*. On 5 December, ENS A. J. Klein had a barrier crash with a SB2C-3 Helldiver. The crash was deemed 100% pilot error, and aircraft Bu. No. 19032 was struck as non-salvageable. Two days later, ENS Klcin had another barrier crash in a SB2C-3. This time, he made a good approach and landing but his tail hook bounced, missing all of the arresting wires. On 11 December, LT(jg) G W. McKenzie landed too far to starboard, caught an arresting wire but slid into starboard catwalk. The propeller and right landing flap on his Helldiver were damaged and the crash was deemed pilot error.

---

[172] U.S. Navy. *USS Charger.* (CVE-30). War Diary November 1944. 1 December 1944. RG38, NARA, Archives II.

[173] U.S. Navy. *USS Charger.* (CVE-30). War Diary November 1944. 1 December 1944. RG38, NARA, Archives II.

Later that day, LT R J. Clinton had a barrier crash. He made a wheels first landing. The plane bounced and the tail hook bounced over wires. Low hydraulic fluid contributed to tail hook bounce. The Helldiver's propeller speed ring and engine fairing were damaged. VB-16 experienced three mishaps on 17 December. ENS E. G. Porupsky had a barrier crash that bent the propeller of his Helldiver. ENS J. P. Onorato experienced a very unusual mishap. On take-off, a tow line fouled in the landing gear of his aircraft. Unbeknownst to him, tow line prevented landing gear from locking into place. Upon landing on *Charger,* the landing gear collapsed. The third mishap of the day did not involve *Charger.* ENS J. S. Chambers went into a dive with his Helldiver. While climbing after the dive, his aircraft's engine suddenly quit. Chambers was able to make a wheels and flaps up belly landing on a nearby beach. ENS Chambers and his aircrewman ARM3C W. H. LeGrand both survive. VB-16's final mishap of the month occurred on 28 December when LT R. N. Mackin had a barrier crash. LT Mackin had a tail high landing. He then bounced his aircraft causing the tail hook to miss the arresting wires. The propeller, landing gear fairing and landing flaps were all damaged.[174]

During the month of December 1944, *Charger* conducted flight operations on eighteen of thirty-one days. 1,578 landings were performed. There were twelve aviation mishaps, six of which were barrier crashes. An aircraft from Composite Squadron Fifteen crashed into *Charger*'s island, through the crash barrier and ended up on the starboard catwalk. Remarkably there were no injuries. Three aircraft were lost in the water but all three pilots were

---

[174] U.S. Navy. Bombing Squadron Sixteen. War Diary 1 Dec 44 to 31 Dec 44. 1 January 1945. RG38, NARA, Archives II.

rescued. On 6 December, an aircraft crashed into the ship's flying bridge, then went over the starboard side into the water. Another aircraft crashed into the water on take-off. Finally, the third aircraft crashed into the water on 27 December.[175]

Composite Squadron Fifteen (VC-15) was a frequent visitor to *USS Charger.* Commissioned on 18 October 1943 at NAS Seattle, Washington, VC-15 came east five months later. The squadron served aboard *USS Croatan* (CVE-25) on anti-submarine patrols in the Atlantic Ocean during the summer and early fall of 1944. Returning to Norfolk in October, VC-15 was re-assigned to training carrier replacement pilots. The squadron frequently worked with *Charger* in this endeavor. Classes arrived on the 1st and 15th of the month and averaged ten weeks of training. There were usually ten torpedo and two fighter pilots in each class. VC-15 operated FM-2 Wildcats and TBM Avengers, both of which were built by General Motors under license from the Grumman Aircraft Company. ENS Maurice J. Lambert was killed during night carrier qualifications. The squadron was decommissioned on 14 June 1945.[176]

---

[175] U.S. Navy. *USS Charger* (CVE-30). War Diary for December 1944. 1 January 1945. RG38, NARA, Archives II.

[176] U.S. Navy. Composite Squadron Fifteen. VC-15. History of Composite Squadron 15. Undated. RG38, NARA, Archives II.

Chapter Ten - Life Aboard Ship

Operating a naval warship was a complicated affair requiring teamwork, organization and discipline. Morale was also highly important to the efficient and effective operation of the ship. Like other U.S. Navy ships, *Charger* had a number of means to maintain morale and keep the ship's company engaged when not on duty or on watch. The ship's Athletic Department coordinated sports and physical activities. Several sports teams competed against teams from other Navy ships and shore commands, including basketball and baseball. Box matches were held amongst the ship's company and sailors and officers competed in a volleyball league aboard ship. Other sports and activities included swimming, touch football, weight lifting and softball.

A Navy chaplain performed religious worship services and offered ministry and counseling to the ship's company. Worship services were frequently held on the Hangar Deck as it provided a large open area protected from the weather and the elements. Both LT(jg) Ralph Thibodeau and Motor Machinists Mate 3rd Class Andrew Futey assisted the Catholic chaplain with Catholic Masses held aboard ship. Given that Thibodeau worked on the flight deck and Futey worked in the engine rooms, this would probably have been the only venue where they may have come in contact with each other.

The ship published its own newspaper. In December 1944, *The Super Charger*'s staff included Editor Seaman 1st Class Don G. Weller, Sports Editor SpA1C R. Nelson, Art Editor ENS C. W. Frey, and Photo Editor Photographers Mate 1st Class W. J. Vallentyne. LT(jg) Ralph A. Thibodeau, LT E. F. Carey, ENS Morton Sonnoborn and Chaplain Blake Craft served as Advisors. *The Super Charger* included messages from ship's leaders, news about the ship's sports teams, and various other items of interest to the ship's company.[177]

The Special Christmas Issue of *The Super Charger* contained greetings and well wishes from the ship's commanding officer CAPT R. R. Johnson, Chaplain Blake Craft and various officers and leaders of the escort carrier. Editor S1C Don Weller penned a parody on the *iconic* "'Twas the Night Before Christmas. CAPT Johnson penned the following short message to his crew.

> It gives me great pleasure to extend to each member of the crew of the CHARGER the best wishes for a Merry Christmas and a Happy and prosperous New Year. You all have earned the greatest present that a good crew can earn ---- the knowledge that you have done an exceptionally fine job throughout the past year. You may all be proud of this, and may you keep up the good work during the coming year. I am proud and happy to have had the privilege of serving with you. You have given me the nicest present I could possibly receive --- your cooperation --- and I thank you so much.

---

[177] U.S. Navy. *USS Charger.* CVE-30. *The Super Charger.* Christmas Issue 1944. My thanks to Ralph Thibodeau Jr. for providing me with a digital copy of this issue.

Chapter Eleven
The Last Year of the War

As 1945 opened, the Allied Forces were heavily engaged in combat operations across the globe. U.S. Army forces were busily involved with liberating the Philippines Archipelago. The U.S. Navy and the U.S. Marine Corps were preparing for the invasions of Iwo Jima and Okinawa. Allied forces were slugging it out with the German Army in northern Italy. In Belgium and Luxembourg, the First and Third U.S. Armies were struggling in heavy snows to repel the surprise German Counter-Offensive. As events were to prove, 1945 would be the final year for the Third Reich and Imperial Japan.

Training Operations in 1945

Even during the winter, *USS Charger* was fully engaged in qualifying pilots for carrier service. The ship conducted flight operations on eighteen days in January 1945. Seven squadrons qualified their pilots aboard *Charger* that month. 1,743 landings were performed. There were also seventeen crashes, either into the barrier or the catwalk. On 3 January 1945, one aircraft crashed into the water off the carrier's port bow while entering the landing circle. The pilot was rescued but the aircraft was not recovered. On two days (13 January and 24 January), *Charger* was host to groups of visitors. Demonstrations of simulated air attacks upon the ship were performed for the visitors on both occasions.[178]

On 3 January 1945, *USS Charger* was host to a most unusual and revolutionary aircraft. The Ryan FR-1 Fireball was the Navy's first aircraft with jet propulsion. On that day, a FR-1 Fireball performed landing and take-off tests aboard the escort carrier.[179]

Torpedo Squadron Eighty-Nine performed carrier qualifications aboard *Charger* in the month of January 1945. The squadron experienced four mishaps, two of which were by the same pilot. On 25 January, ENS H W. Roesener crashed his Avenger because tail hook did not fully extend. The next day, the tail hook on ENS E. Malm's Avenger pulled out on landing. ENS T. R. Robertson had the dubious distinction of crashing and seriously damaging two Avengers. On 18 January, he experienced a hard landing that required a major overhaul of his Avenger. Then while performing night qualifications on 31 January, ENS Robertson came in too fast for the landing. His aircraft bounced, caught the next to last wire but still hit the island and the crash barrier. There were no injuries but the aircraft required a major overhaul afterwards.[180]

---

[178] U.S. Navy. *USS Charger.* CVE-30 War Diary for January 1945. 1 February 1945. RG38, NARA, Archives II.

[179] "Catapult-Fire!" *Naval Aviation News.* (August 1946). See photo on page 18.; U.S. Navy. *USS Charger.* CVE-30 War Diary for January 1945. 1 February 1945. RG38, NARA, Archives II.

[180] U.S. Navy. Torpedo Squadron Eighty-Nine. War Diary for January 1945. 1 February 1945. RG38, NARA, Archives II.

Charger was no less busy in February 1945. She conducted flight operations on 19 of 28 days that month. Pilots from eight squadrons, including two from the British Royal Navy, performed 1,710 day and night landings aboard her. There were seven crashes, of which three aircraft ended up in the bay and were lost. Fortunately no one was killed in any of these mishaps.[181]

One of the eight squadrons training with *Charger* in February 1945 was U.S. Navy Bombing Squadron Eighty-Nine. Bombing Eighty-Nine had begun qualifying its pilots in January and by 20 February, all of its pilots had been qualified in both day and night landings. The following month on 21 March, the squadron embarked aboard *USS Antietam* (CV-36) and headed west for the Pacific War.[182]

In the month of March 1945, *Charger* conducted flight operations on 24 of the month's 31 days. A total of fourteen squadrons, including two from the British Royal Navy, performed carrier qualifications aboard the escort carrier. 2,773 landings were performed that month. Sixteen mishaps occurred during the month. Most of these mishaps were crashes into the barrier or the starboard or port catwalks with minor damage to ship and aircraft and minor injuries to the pilots. Three were three mishaps, however, in which the aircraft was lost. On 28 March, an aircraft crashed on take-off. The plane was lost but the pilot was

---

[181] U.S. Navy. *USS Charger.* CVE-30 War Diary for Febuary 1945. 1 March 1945. RG38, NARA, Archives II.

[182] U.S. Navy. Bombing Squadron Elghty-Nine. War History. 23 April 1946.

recovered. Another aircraft went over the side on landing. Again, the plane was lost but the pilot was rescued.[183]

The most serious mishap of the month and of the year to date involved a F4U Corsair piloted by Ensign John A. Hafner, USNR, of Navy Bomber-Fighter Squadron One Hundred Fifty. On 31 March 1945, VBF-150 was performing carrier qualifications. The squadron was commanded by LCDR C. S. Radford, Jr. ENS Hafner had 419.7 flight hours, including 74.7 in the Corsair. At around 1300, Hafner was in the landing pattern for *Charger.* He was high on the downwind leg of the pattern. When he turned into the cross-wind leg, his aircraft went into a steep nose down turn. The Corsair spun left out of the turn and struck the water. Hafner was killed. He was the squadron's first fatality.[184]

In the month of April 1945, *USS Charger* conducted flight operations on nineteen of the month's thirty days. During that time, *Charger* had a total of 2,659 day and night landings. On most days, day landings far surpassed night landings. On 21 April, however, the numbers were nearly equal. Fighter-Bomber Squadron 150 performed 89 day landings and 81 night landings, and qualified forty of its pilots. There were eleven aircraft crashes with two aircraft going overboard and into the water. On 7 April, an aircraft missed the arresting wires, struck the upper wire of the

---

[183] U.S. Navy. *USS Charger.* CVE-30 War Diary for March 1945. 1 April 1945. RG38, NARA, Archives II.

[184] *USS Charger.* War Diary for March 1945; U.S. Navy. Bombing Fighter Squadron One Hundred Fifty. War Diary 1 March to 31 March 1945. 2 April 1945. RG38, NARA, Archives II.

crash barrier and went into the water off the port bow. The pilot was rescued; the plane was a total loss. On 15 April, a F6F Hellcat broke its tail hook while attempting to land. The Hellcat then bounced over the barrier, and into the water off the starboard bow. The pilot was rescued. He sustained a moderate concussion and minor scalp lacerations. The aircraft was not recovered.[185]

Eleven squadrons trained aboard *Charger* in the month of April 1945. Among these was Navy Fighting Squadron Twenty-Seven. The squadron was placed in commission at Naval Air Station Alameda, California on 15 October 1943. Assigned to the light aircraft carrier *USS Princeton* (CVL-22), VF-27 participated in the Marianas Invasion, the Battle of the Philippine Sea, the Philippines invasion and the Battle of the Leyte Gulf. On 24 October 1943, *Princeton* was sunk by a Japanese air attack. The surviving members of VF-27 returned to the United States. On 2 January 1945, the squadron was reformed at Naval Auxiliary Airfield Sanford, Maine. In April 1945, VF-27 performed carrier landing qualifications aboard *Charger.* The following June, VF-27 embarked aboard *USS Independence* (CVL-23). As part of Task Group 38.4, *Independence* and VF-27 participated in air strikes on the Japanese Home Islands in July and August. On the day that the

---

[185] U.S. Navy. *USS Charger.* CVE-30 War Diary for April 1945. 1 May 1945. RG38, NARA, Archives II.

Japanese surrendered, *Independence* was among the U.S. ships anchored in Tokyo Bay for the proceedings.[186]

Bombing Fighting Squadron One Hundred Fifty-One was equipped with F4U Corsairs. The squadron experienced seven mishaps during its carrier qualifications aboard *Charger* in the month of April 1945. Five of these mishaps involved tail wheel collapses, which was a notorious problem for the Corsair. First on 18 April, LT (jg) Rox caught the number #3 arresting wire but the wire broke and damaged his Corsair's tail assembly. There were two mishaps the following day. LT G B Riley damaged his Corsair's tail assembly, and its tail wheel collapsed. ENS Mark T. Nevill damaged the starboard wing on his Corsair when his plane swerved into *Charger's* island. On 28 April, four VBF-151 Corsairs suffered damaged from collapsing tail wheels. These aircraft were piloted by LT (jg) R. L. Laskey, and Ensigns R. A. Harwood, E B Tomczak and M T. Nevill.[187]

In month of May 1945, the war in Europe came to an end. Since Adolf Hitler committed suicide in his bunker in Berlin on 30 April 1945, it fell to other Nazi leaders to effectuate the surrender of the Third Reich to the Allies. By this time, Germany had been completely overrun by the British, Canadian, American, French and Soviet armies.

---

[186] U.S. Navy. Fighting Squadron Twenty-Seven. History of Fighting Squadron Twenty-Seven. 15 October 1943 - 1 March 1945. RG38, NARA, Archives II.; U.S. Navy. Fighting Squadron Twenty-Seven. History of Fighting Squadron Twenty-Seven. 26 October 1945. RG38, NARA, Archives II.

[187] U.S. Navy. Bombing Fighting Squadron One Hundred Fifty. War Diary. 1 May to 31 May 1945. 1 June 1945. RG38, NARA. Archives II.

The war in the Pacific, however, continued unabated. The invasion of Okinawa entered its second deadly month. On land, U.S. Marines and soldiers fought vicious battles against heavily dug in Japanese defenders. Off shore, U.S. sailors fought life and death struggles against relentless Japanese kamikaze attacks.

Flight operations aboard *USS Charger* in May 1945 were very busy. On both 1 May and 5 May, 187 day landings were performed on each day. During the first two weeks of May 1945, *Charger* conducted 1,327 landings, of which 130 were at night. In those first two weeks, 179 pilots were carrier-qualified, including 18 pilots from Royal Navy Squadron No. 738. U.S. Navy squadrons that conducted qualifications aboard Charger during this time included VBF-151, VT-150, VF-28 and VB-151.[188]

In the Chesapeake Bay, training operations continued aboard *USS Charger.* Flight operations were conducted on twenty-one days that month. 1,729 successful landings were performed in May by pilots of fourteen U.S. Navy squadrons and one Royal Navy squadron. VADM P. N. L. Bellinger, Commander of Naval Air Forces Atlantic, came aboard *Charger* on 18 May to observe flight operations. There were five barrier crashes, three aircraft broke landing gear while landing, and two aircraft were lost in the waters of the Chesapeake Bay. On 5 May, an aircraft attempting to land was waved off and spun into the water. The plane was lost but the pilot was recovered. On 21 May, a SB2C from Bombing Squadron One Hundred Fifty-One took a wave off and then crashed into the water off the port side. Both pilot ENS Daniel Francis Malloy Jr. and his aircraft were lost. Malloy's body was not recovered. ENS

---

[188] See *Charger* War Diary for May 1945.

Malloy was one of five children born to Daniel Francis Malloy and the former Emily H. Dixon of Worcester, Massachusetts. He was twenty-years-old.

There were other less serious mishaps aboard *USS Charger* in May 1945 as pilots made mistakes and equipment failed. Both occurred on 5 May 1945. Two aircraft caught the arresting wires but then their landing gear collapsed. Another aircraft missed the arresting wires altogether and crashed into the cable barrier. Yet another aircraft broke its tail hook while landing and also crashed into the barrier. No personnel were injured and each plane suffered only minor damage. The most serious mishap occurred when a pilot was waved off from landing and crashed into the water. The plane was lost but the pilot only suffered minor abrasions.[189]

ENS D. R. Gerberding of Torpedo Squadron One Hundred Fifty had two barrier crashes aboard *Charger* in the month of May. One occurred in the daytime and the other occurred at night. ENS Gerberding had 450 total flight hours, including 200 hours in Avengers.[190]

May 1945 was a very difficult month for Bombing Fighting Squadron One Hundred Fifty (VBF-150). While performing carrier qualifications, the squadron experienced five mishaps aboard *Charger.* On 16 May, the starboard landing gear collapsed

---

[189] See War Diary for 5 May 1945.; U.S. Navy. Bombing Squadron One Hundred Fifty-One. War Diary for May 1945. 1 June 1945. RG38, NARA, Archives II.

[190] U.S. Navy. Torpedo Squadron One Hundred Fifty. War Diary for May 1945. RG 38, NARA, Archives II.

on ENS H. W. Baird's F4U Corsair while attempting a night landing on *Charger.* The next day, LT Boyd N. Mayhew's Corsair experienced a collapsed tail wheel assembly. On 22 May, the tail wheel assembly on ENS R. A. Mumert's Corsair collapsed during a night landing and Ensigns R. R. Mercer and R. A. Harwood had barrier crashes.[191]

Ashore, VBF-150's luck was even worse. On 19 May 1945, a VBF-150 pilot ground looped his SNJ at NAS Roosevelt Field. Tragedy struck on 27 May. ENS John F. Darcy experienced a flight emergency while flying a SNJ over western Pennsylvania. He attempted to land his SNJ at the municipal airport in Dubois, Pennsylvania but crashed and was severely injured. He was taken to Dubois's Maple Avenue Hospital for treatment. Later that day, the Squadron Flight Officer LT L. C. Flynt flew an SNJ up from NAAS Oceana, Virginia with a passenger to investigate ENS Dubois's crash. Nearing his destination, LT Flynt experienced a flight emergency and had to make a forced landing on a highway southeast of Dubois. Neither he nor his passenger were injured but there was serious damage to the SNJ. Then on 29 May, ENS Darcy died in the hospital from his injuries.[192]

John F. Darcy was born on 12 August 1922 in Rochester, New York to Mr. and Mrs. George Darcy. He had two brothers, Milton and George. After graduating from West High School where he played basketball and golf, John went to work for the Kodak

---

[191] U.S. Navy. Bombing Fighting Squadron One Hundred Fifty. War Diary. 1 May to 31 May 1945. 1 June 1945. RG38, NARA, Archives II.

[192] U.S. Navy. Bombing Fighting Squadron One Hundred Fifty. War Diary. 1 May to 31 May 1945. 1 June 1945. RG38, NARA, Archives II.

Company. Darcy entered the Naval Aviation Cadet program on 9 October 1942 and earned his Naval Aviator Wings. His two brothers also joined the war effort. Milton enlisted in the U.S. Army and George was commissioned in the Navy Reserve. John Darcy returned home to Rochester where a Funeral Mass was offered for him at Immaculate Conception Church on Friday 1 June 1945. Afterwards he was interred at Holy Sepulchre Cemetery.[193]

Navy Fighting Squadron One Hundred Fifty-Three performed carrier qualifications aboard *Charger* in June 1945. They had four mishaps during those qualifications. The first two mishaps occurred on 10 June. ENS R. M. Warfel crashed his F6F-5 Hellcat into the crash barrier and damaged its propeller. On 20 June, ENS J. R. Thomas crashed his F6F-5 Hellcat into the barrier and damaged its propeller. VF-153 While attempting to land the next day, ENS E. G. Clouser hit the flight deck with the propeller of his Hellcat, damaging the propeller. The most serious mishap, however, occurred on 10 June. While attempting to land aboard *Charger,* ENS H. R. Maier went over the side of the ship and into the water. His F6F-5 Hellcat was lost but he was rescued. He sustained only minor injuries.[194]

Navy Fighting Bombing Squadron One Hundred Fifty-Three performed carrier qualifications aboard *Charger* in June 1945.

---

[193] "Ensign John F. Darcy." *Democrat and Chronicle* (Rochester, NY). May 30, 1945: pg. 7.

[194] U.S. Navy. Fighting Squadron One Hundred Fifty-Three. War Diary. June 1945. 1 July 1945. RG38, NARA, Archives II.

They had six mishaps. On 19 June, LT(jg) W. W. Tyler got the tail hook of his F4U Corsair caught on the aft elevator flange, snapping it off. He then crashed into the barrier. That same day, ENS F. E. Morris wrecked his Corsair while landing aboard the ship. Three days later, LT(jg) John W. Eash was attempting a night landing. He came in too high, over compensated too much and nosed down too much. His front wheels hit the deck first, which caused his Corsair to bounce. Though he managed to catch the last arresting wire, he still careened into the barrier. On 24 June, LT(jg) W W Tyler had his second mishap of the month. While attempting a night landing, he landed slightly too far to port. Though he managed to catch the Number Two arresting wire, he dropped a wheel into the port catwalk. While performing a night landing on 27 June, LT(jg) William H. Gregory caught the last arresting wire which broke and sent his Corsair into the barrier. Finally on 29 June, ENS Charles V. Lanier damaged his tail post assembly when landed with his front wheels first.[195]

In the month of July 1945, *Charger* had only 525 landings but these were all performed in just three days of flight operations. *Charger* steamed to the operating area on 2 July and conducted flight operations for VBF-20, VBF-93, VF-153, VBF-153 and VT-20 until 4 July. On 5 July, CAPT R. R. Johnson was relieved by CAPT W. M. Walsh. *Charger* spent the remainder of the month at Navy Yard Norfolk for maintenance and overhaul work.[196]

---

[195] U.S. Navy. Fighting Bombing Squadron One Hundred Fifty-Three. War Diary. June 1945. 1 July 1945. RG38, NARA, Archives II.

[196] U.S. Navy. *USS Charger.* CVE-30 War Diary for July 1945. 1 August 1945. RG38, NARA, Archives II.

Preparations were well underway for the climactic invasion of the Japanese Home Islands. Ground divisions of the U.S. Army and aviation units of the U.S. Army Air Forces were redeploying from the European Theater back to the United States in preparation for the upcoming invasion of Kyushu, Operation Olympic, scheduled for November. Both this invasion and the planned invasion of Honshu, Operation Coronet, would be the most massive amphibious assault in history. Unbeknownst all but the senior most American and British military and political leaders and scientists, the United States had been developing a secret weapon to end the war. On 6 August 1945, a B-29 Superfortress from Tinian Island dropped an atomic bomb on the city of Hiroshima, unleashing unprecedented destruction. Japanese leaders were unconvinced by the fury of the bomb, and so, a second atomic bomb had to be dropped. This one devastated the city of Nagasaki. Then the Soviet Union declared war on Japan and launched a massive operation in Manchuria. Fending off a last minute coup by Japanese military officers, Emperor Hirohito and the senior political and military leaders of Japan announced their willingness to surrender and thus end World War Two.[197]

LT Thibodeau was aboard *Charger* when he learned of the atomic bombs being dropped on Hiroshima and Nagasaki. "All I knew was the war was over, and I could head for home," he later recalled.[198]

There was no mention of any of these events in the War Diary. During this fateful time, *USS Charger* was moored to the port side

---

[197] U.S. Navy. *USS Charger.* CVE-30 War Diary for August 1945. 1 September 1945. RG38, NARA, Archives II.

[198] Quoted in Ralph A. Thibodeau Jr.'s biography of his father.

of Berth 43 at the Norfolk Navy Yard in Portsmouth, Virginia. She spent nearly the entire month of August in port undergoing repairs. *Charger* got underway on 27 August for post-repair trials and then returned to Berth 43 later that day. She remained there for two more days, then moved over first to the Craney Island Pier and then to the south side of Pier Number 5, Berth 56 at Naval Operating Base Norfolk. Here she moored until 4 September.[199]

The Empire of Japan formally surrendered to the Allied Powers on the deck of the battleship *USS Missouri* (BB-63) in Tokyo Bay on 2 September 1945. Though she had never fired a shot in anger nor launched any air missions against Japan, *Charger* had played an important role in the achievement of the Victory over Japan. Pilots trained aboard *Charger* had fired shots in anger and had conducted combat missions against Japanese forces.

On the historic day of the Japanese Surrender, *Charger* was moored to the south side of Pier Number 5, Berth Number 56, at Naval Operating Base, Norfolk, Virginia. Though the ship's War Diary only recorded "Moored as before," it can be expected that the news of the Japanese surrender came with great relief for the crew of *USS Charger.*[200]

Nevertheless, *Charger* had a mission to perform, that of training pilots in carrier landings and take-offs. Two days later at 0906, *Charger* cast off her lines and got underway for the operating area. Only four landings were performed that day. One SNJ crashed into

---

[199] U.S. Navy. *USS Charger.* CVE-30 War Diary for August 1945. 1 September 1945. RG38, NARA, Archives II.

[200] U.S. Navy. *USS Charger* (CVE-30). War Diary for September 1945. 1 October 1945. RG38, NARA, Archives II.

the barrier, resulting in minor damage to the aircraft but fortunately no injuries to pilot or ship's crew. *Charger* anchored in the operating overnight and then resumed flight operations the following day. Bombing Squadron Seventy-Five performed 49 landings that day. On 6 September, only three landings were performed but a VB-75 Helldiver crashed into the barrier. Also, a sailor fell overboard. He was rescued uninjured. That night *Charger* tested new deck lighting during night carrier operations. Flight operations resumed on 10 September but only two landings occurred. On 11 September, Torpedo Squadron Seventy-Five joined its sister squadron for carrier landings. 140 successful landings were performed that day.[201]

Both VB-75 and VT-75 were part of Air Group 75 which was assigned to the brand new aircraft carrier *USS Franklin D. Roosevelt* (CVB-42). Originally named *USS Coral Sea, USS Franklin D. Roosevelt* had been renamed for the late president. The new carrier was the second of the new *Midway*-class of large aircraft carriers. Ultimately, there would be three *Midway*-class aircraft carriers: *Midway* (CVB-41), *Franklin D. Roosevelt* (CVB-42), and *Coral Sea* (CVB-43). *Midway* and *Coral Sea* would see service well into the 1990s. The *Midway*-class carriers displaced 45,000 tons, and had a length of 968 feet, a beam of 113 feet, a flight deck width of 136 feet, and a draft of 35 feet. They could carry upwards of 144 aircraft. *Midway* was placed in commission on 10 September 1945; *Franklin D. Roosevelt* would be placed in commission on 27 October 1945. Compared with *Charger*'s 410-foot long flight deck, Air Group 75's pilots would

---

[201] U.S. Navy. *USS Charger* (CVE-30). War Diary for September 1945. 1 October 1945. RG38, NARA, Archives II.

feel like they were landing aboard a naval air station runway when they landed aboard *Franklin D. Roosevelt.*[202]

On 12 September, both squadrons performed a total of 147 landings aboard *Charger.* Unfortunately, VB-75 suffered a fatal aviation mishap. One of its Helldivers was in the landing circle when it unexpectedly crashed into the water ahead of *Charger.* Neither the pilot nor the aircraft were recovered.[203]

A total of 140 landings were performed on 13 September and 70 landings were performed on 14 September. That ended flight operations for September. That month, 519 carrier landings performed in just eight days of flight operations. There were also three mishaps, one of which resulted in the loss of a VB-75 Helldiver and its pilot. Torpedo Squadron Seventy-five performed its qualifications without a single mishap. As the Squadron's War Diary recorded, "The main accomplishment during the month was the checking out of twenty-six pilots aboard the U.S.S. CHARGER without any mishaps, earning the squadron a 'Well Done' from the Captain of the ship."[204]

---

[202] See *Dictionary of American Naval Fighting Ships* entry for *USS Franklin D. Roosevelt,* accessed online on 15 June 2020 at https://www.history.navy.mil/research/histories/ship-histories/danfs/f/franklin-d-roosevelt-cvb-42.html

[203] U.S. Navy. *USS Charger* (CVE-30). War Diary for September 1945. 1 October 1945. RG38, NARA, Archives II.

[204] U.S. Navy. *USS Charger* (CVE-30). War Diary for September 1945. 1 October 1945. RG38, NARA, Archives II.; U.S. Navy. Air Group Seventy-Five. Torpedo Squadron Seventy-Five. War Diary for September 1945. 1 October 1945. RG38, NARA, Archives II.

Guantanamo Bay

On 18 September, *Charger* got underway for only her second oceanic voyage. She departed Naval Operating Base Norfolk to transport passengers and cargo for the Navy's base at Guantanamo Bay, Cuba. This was Fireman 2nd Class Andy Futey's one and only ocean voyage.[205]

Guantanamo Bay was a Navy logistics base located on the southeast corner of Cuba. U.S. forces had seized the bay during the Spanish-American War and set up a forward base there. The United States formalized the base in December 1903 by leasing forty-five square miles of land and water area from the new Cuba Republic. A 1934 Treaty re-affirmed the lease and modified the lease payment. Naval Station Guantanamo Bay supported Navy operations in the Caribbean Sea throughout World War Two. NS Guantanamo Bay remained in U.S. use even after the 1959 Communist Revolution. The 1934 Treaty required both parties to agree to terminate the lease, and so the United States has used that provision to retain the base. During the Global War on Terrorism, NS Guantanamo Bay was used to detain captured enemy combatants.[206]

On 22 September, Charger anchored at Berth Number 37 at Guantanamo Bay and began unloading her passengers and cargo. Charger's visit to Cuba was brief. She completed unloading the next day. At 0658 on 24 September, she got underway for the

---

[205] U.S. Navy. *USS Charger* (CVE-30). War Diary for September 1945. 1 October 1945. RG38, NARA, Archives II.

[206] U.S. Navy. Commander, Navy Region Southeast. Naval Station Guantanamo Bay. History. Accessed online on 15 June 2020 at https://www.cnic.navy.mil/regions/cnrse/installations/ns_guantanamo_bay/about/history.html

return voyage to NOB Norfolk. At 1229 on 27 September, she tied up to the northside of Pier Number 7, Berth Number 75 at NOB Norfolk.[207]

After Guantanamo Bay

For the first nine days of October 1945, *Charger* was either moored to a pier at NOB Norfolk or anchored in Hampton Roads. On 6 October, she transferred thirty-three sailors to the Personnel Separation Center for discharge from active duty. On 9 October, Task Unit 21.8.1 was constituted by COMAIRLANT (Commander, Naval Air Forces Atlantic). *Charger*'s commanding officer, CAPT William W. Walsh, was designated as the Task Unit Commander. Escort Division 79 was assigned to TU 21.8.1 for escort and plane guard duty. Escort Division 79 consisted of *USS Carter* (DE-112), *USS Neal A. Scott* (DE-769), *USS Muir* (DE-770) and *USS Sutton* (DE-771). *Charger* conducted flight operations periodically throughout October. On 10 October, Torpedo Squadron 75 performed eighty-seven day landings and qualified six of its pilots. On 29 October, Escort Division 54 relieved Escort Division 79. Escort Division 54 was comprised of *USS Francis M. Robinson* (DE-220), *USS Solar* (DE-221) and *USS Fowler (*DE-222).[208]

Charger was either moored to a pier at NOB Norfolk or anchored in Hampton Roads for the first two weeks of November. On 3 November, seventy-four sailors were transferred to the Personnel Separation Center for discharge from Naval Service. She did not get underway for flight operations until 15 November. In those last

---

[207] U.S. Navy. *USS Charger* (CVE-30). War Diary for September 1945. 1 October 1945. RG38, NARA, Archives II.

[208] U.S. Navy. USS *Charger* (CVE-30). War Diary 1 OCT 1945 to 31 OCT 1945. 1 November 1945. RG38, NARA, Archives II.

two weeks or so of November, *Charger* performed 739 landings. There were five aviation mishaps that month, involving three F6F Hellcats and a TBM Avenger. At 1245 on 29 November, ENS Robert A. Scott of Torpedo Squadron 43 made the 50,000[th] landing aboard the escort carrier.[209]

Charger began the month of December 1945 still as part of Task Unit 21.8.1. Her commanding officer, CAPT William M. Walsh, remained as Task Unit Commander. On 7 December, CAPT Walsh was replaced as Task Unit Commander by CAPT John P. Fitzsimmons of *USS Mission Bay* (CVE-59). The month was somewhat confusing for *Charger.* On 14 December, she reported to Commander, Inactive Fleet, Atlantic Fleet and her status was to be "In Commission, In Reserve." *Charger* would then be assigned to the Boston Group, Inactive Fleet. These orders were subsequently cancelled. Instead, *Charger* was ordered to report to Commandant, Third Naval District for decommissioning.[210]

At some point, *Charger* made her way to New York. She was decommissioned there on 15 March 1946. Nearly a year later, *Charger* was sold on 30 January 1947.[211]

---

[209] U.S. Navy. *USS Charger* (CVE-30). War Diary 1 NOV 1945 to 30 NOV 1945. 1 December 1945. RG38, NARA, Archives II.

[210] U.S. Navy. *USS Charger.* (CVE-30). War Diary 1 December 1945 to 31 December 1945. 1 January 1946. RG38, NARA, Archives II.

[211] See *USS Charger* entry in the *Dictionary of American Naval Fighting Ships* accessed online at https://www.history.navy.mil/research/histories/ship-histories/danfs/c/charger.html

Chapter Twelve
Charger After the War

Charger continued training pilots through the end of 1945. In September 1945, *Charger* undertook her second and final voyage outside the Chesapeake Bay when she ferried aircraft to the Naval Base at Guantanamo Bay, Cuba. Fireman 2nd Class Futey undertook the voyage.[212]

By 1946, the U.S. Navy no longer had a need for the small escort carrier. On 15 March 1946, she was decommissioned at New York. She was sold to the Sitmar Shipping Line on 30 January 1947. After major renovations which included removing her flight deck, *Charger* was converted to a passenger liner capable of accommodating 1,800 passengers and re-named *Fairsea*. She was the line's first passenger ship. Sitmar Lines obtained a contract from the International Refugee Organization (IRO) to transport war refugees and immigrants from Europe to Australia for re-settlement. On 3 December 1949, she departed Genoa, Italy on her first voyage transporting immigrants and arrived in Sydney, Australia on 30 December 1949.[213]

---

[212] See DANFS entry for *USS Charger.*

[213] See DANFS entry for *USS Charger.;* "Post World War II Immigrant Ships: Fairsea." Museum Victoria Fact Sheet (2007). Found online at http://museumvictoria.com.au/DiscoveryCentre/Infosheets/Fairsea/

Fairsea's accommodations were far from luxurious. Because sleeping arrangements were in open spaces with triple-decked bunks, male and female passengers were berthed separately. Toilet and shower facilities were communal. There were no private cabins for passengers.[214]

In 1955, the Australia government chartered *Fairsea* to transport immigrants from Britain. She continued in this service until going in for an extensive renovation and refit in October 1957. *Fairsea*'s refit lasted six months. During this time, major improvements were made to the berthing accommodations, air conditioning was installed, and her overall external appearance dramatically changed. Following her refit, *Fairsea* re-entered charter service with the Australian government and New Zealand was included in her destinations. Altogether from 1949 to 1969, *Fairsea* made 81 voyages to and from Australia.[215]

One of those immigrants from the United Kingdom to Australia was Paul Trangmar. In January 1964, nine-year-old Paul, his parents and siblings boarded *Fairsea* for the voyage to their new home in Australia. By now, *Fairsea*'s berthing accommodations had been much improved. Paul and his family stayed in a cabin on the Boat Deck just below the Bridge Deck. Years later, he recalled his voyage to a new life in Australia aboard *Fairsea* (ex-*USS Charger*):

---

[214] "Post World War II Immigrant Ships: Fairsea." Museum Victoria Fact Sheet (2007). Found online at http://museumvictoria.com.au/ DiscoveryCentre/Infosheets/Fairsea/

[215] "Post World War II Immigrant Ships: Fairsea." Museum Victoria Fact Sheet (2007). Found online at http://museumvictoria.com.au/ DiscoveryCentre/Infosheets/Fairsea/

I had the great fortune to voyage in *Fairsea* with my parents and siblings from UK to our new home in Australia in Jan/Feb 1964. While just 9 at the time, my memories of the trip are vivid and helped shaped my subsequent career first the Australian Navy, later in the British Merchant Service. While on that voyage I became aware that *Fairsea* had once been an escort aircraft carrier vital to training aircrews for the Allied war effort, also that her 'newer' sister *Fairsky* had very similar construction origins. I was further lucky enough to visit the engine-room with my father, who had struck up a friendship with *Fairsea*'s Chief Engineer. I then learned that the 'Chief' had served in the Italian Navy submarines during WW2, the irony of same only later dawning on me with maturity.[216]

Fairsea's sea service abruptly came to an end in 1969. While west of Panama, she suffered a major fire in her engine room which destroyed much of the machinery. She turned back to Panama and remained at Balboa while her fate was decided. Ultimately, it was decided that the damage was too extensive and that her advanced age was not worth the expense of repairs. She was sold for scrap and on 9 July 1969, she left Panama bound for the ship breakers at La Spezia, Italy. Later that summer, *MS Rio de la Plata* / *HMS Charger* / *USS Charger* / *Fairsea* was broken up and scrapped.[217]

---

[216] Paul Trangmar. Email to the Author. 19 March 2019.

[217] "Post World War II Immigrant Ships: Fairsea." Museum Victoria Fact Sheet (2007). Found online at http://museumvictoria.com.au/ DiscoveryCentre/Infosheets/Fairsea/

Chapter Thirteen
Charger's Sailors and Pilots After the War

The sailors and airmen who served or trained aboard *USS Charger* had diverse experiences after their time with her.

After relief as commanding officer of *USS Charger,* CAPT Sprague then reported to Commander, Carrier Replacement Squadrons – Atlantic Fleet for duty involving flying as Aide and Chief of Staff. He commissioned *USS Intrepid* (CV-11) in August of 1943 and commanded her during campaigns throughout the Pacific during the first half of 1944. Promoted to Rear Admiral in June 1944, Sprague was placed in command of Carrier Division 22 and Task Group 77.4. On 25 October 1944, he commanded TG77.4 during the Battle off Samar against a powerful force of Japanese surface warships which included the super battleship *Yamato.* He was awarded the Navy Cross for this battle. He next commanded Carrier Division 3 during the Okinawa invasion. Then he commanded Task Force 38.1 for the final air strikes against the Japanese Home Islands. After the war, Rear Admiral Sprague served as Chief of the Bureau of Naval Personnel. Promoted to Vice Admiral, he was appointed Commander of the Pacific Fleet

Air Force and held the post until retiring in April 1952. He passed away in California on 17 September 1972.[218]

CDR Tom Blackburn commanded Fighting Squadron Seventeen in the south Pacific campaigns. Flying F4U Corsairs from shore bases, his VF-17 amassed one of the highest aerial victory totals for the entire war. Eleven VF-17 pilots became aces including Blackburn. Several VF-17 formed the nucleus of Fighting Squadron Eighty-Four which flew Corsairs off *USS Bunker Hill* (CV-17) in the final year of the war. VF-17 Executive Officer LCDR Roger Hedrick served as commanding officer of VF-84. Blackburn remained in naval aviation after the war. He served as the Commander of the aircraft carrier *USS Midway* (CV-41) air group and later as her commanding officer. He retired from the Navy in 1962 at the rank of Captain. He died from cancer in March 1994 and was buried in Arlington National Cemetery.[219]

After commanding *Charger,* CAPT Ralph Woods commanded NAS Daytona Beach, Florida from September 1944 to October 1945, the Navy Pre-Flight School at St. Mary's College, California from November 1945 to May 1946. From June 1946 to August 1947, he commanded the the U.S. Naval Operation Base and Naval Air Station at Midway Island. His next assignment was with Headquarters U.S. Navy at the Pentagon from October 1947 to November 1950. Capt Woods served as commanding officer of the light aircraft carrier *USS Saipan* (CVL-48) from December

---

[218] Morison, *Leyte June 1944 to January 1945,* footnote 16 on page 125.

[219] See Blackburn's memoirs *The Jolly Rogers: The Story of Tom Blackburn and Navy Fighting Squadron VF-17* for more details. Additional information is from his Obituary published 6 April 1994 in the *New York Times.*

1950 to November 1951, and then served as commanding officer of Utility Wing, Pacific, from December 1951 until his retirement from the Navy on July 1, 1953. Ralph Woods died on August 10, 1982, and was buried at the Fort Rosecrans National Cemetery in San Diego, California.[220]

In January 1944, Rear Admiral Oldendorf assumed command of Cruiser Division Four in the Pacific Theater. He subsequently commanded Battleship Division Two and was serving as Commander, Support Force, on 25 October 1944 when his force of battleships, cruisers and destroyers annihilated a Japanese surface force that included two battleships in the Battle of Surigao Strait.[221]

CDR Ahroon left *Charger* in October 1943 and helped fit out another escort carrier, *USS White Plains* (CVE-66). Upon her commissioning on 15 November 1943, CDR Ahroon became her Executive Officer. He served as such during campaigns in the Pacific Theater. During the Saipan Invasion, he was transferred to *USS Lexington* (CV-16) and served as her Executive Officer until the Japanese surrender in September 1945. He was promoted to Captain on 25 March 1945. His post-war assignments included command of the seaplane tender *USS Norton Sound* (AVM-1),

---

[220] U.S. Navy Pre-Flight School. St. Mary's College, California. War Diary 1 to 30 November 1945. RG38, NARA, Archives II.; Ralph W. D. Woods Veteran Tribute http://www.veterantributes.org/TributeDetail.php?recordID=990

[221] "Jesse Barrett Oldendorf   16 February 1887 - 27 April 1974." U.S. Naval History and Heritage Command. Accessed online on 10 September 2020 at https://www.history.navy.mil/research/library/research-guides/modern-biographical-files-ndl/modern-bios-o/oldendorf-jesse-barrett.html

completion of the Industrial College of the Armed Forces, command of Carrier Division Seven, and command of *USS Leyte* (CV-32). At the time of his command of her *Norton Sound* was testing guided missiles. Promoted to Rear Admiral 1 August 1956, he commanded a Hunter-Killer Task Group of the U.S. Seventh Fleet in the Far East on two occasions. In 1960, he served as Commander, Naval Forces, Continental Air Defense Command in Colorado. He died on 26 January 1972.[222]

After the war, LT Thibodeau left Active Duty but remained in the Navy Reserve. He, wife Betty and daughter Carmen resided in St. Paul, Minnesota where he went back to work for the *Catholic Digest* and finished his bachelor's degree at St. Thomas College. In 1948, they relocated to Corpus Christi, Texas. There he studied Voice and Choral at Del Mar College for two years and taught General Music and Choir at a public junior high school. From 1951 to 1956, he taught at College Academy, a private boys Catholic high school. In August 1952, he earned a Masters of Music Education at Texas A&I University in Brownsville. In 1956, Del Mar College hired him to teach Music History, Music Literature, and Italian, German and French for the voice students. He retired from the Navy Reserve in 1960. Over the course of his naval career, LT Thibodeau accumulated five hundred hours of flight time, most of which was performed in the SNJ Texan advanced trainer aircraft. He also flew the N2S-2 and N2S-3 "Yellow Peril," the Douglas SBD Dauntless dive bomber, the Grumman F6F Hellcat fighter, and the Curtiss SOC-4 Seagull float plane. Ralph served as a Professor at Del Mar College until retiring in 1986. He and Betty had three more children: sons

---

[222] U.S. Navy. Office of Information. Biographies Branch. "Rear Admiral Thomas A. Ahroon – United States Navy." 31 March 1960.

Ralph Jr. and John (Jack) and another daughter Renee. Betty passed away in 1986 and Ralph passed away in 2006 at age 84.[223]

In the fall of 1945, Andrew Futey was promoted to Motor Machinists Mate 3rd Class. Later that fall, he was transferred from *USS Charger*. Afterwards, MoMM3c Futey was offered a promotion and a position maintaining the Navy's decommissioned (mothballed) ships berthed near Bear Mountain on the Hudson River in New York. He declined the offer. Futey was discharged from the Navy on 7 December 1945 at USN Personnel Separation Center, Lido Beach, Long Island, New York. He and his family returned to New Jersey.[224]

Over the years, he and Emily would add another son (John) and two daughters (Elaine and Arleen) to their family. They eventually settled in Port Reading, New Jersey. Futey worked in the trucking industry for the next three decades. After that worked in a hospital until his retirement. Ultimately his family would grow to include six grandchildren and eight great-grandchildren. His years in the Navy were a source of great pride to him and he would often recall his time in service fondly.

After a prolonged illness, Andrew Futey passed away on 31 October 2001. A Catholic Memorial Mass was said for him at the Church of St. Elizabeth of Hungary in Carteret, New Jersey. A Navy honor guard participated at his interment. He is buried in the Brigadier General William C. Doyle New Jersey Veterans

---

[223] This paragraph is from Ralph S. Thibodeau Jr.'s August 2020 biography of his father.

[224] Discharge information provided by Futey's personnel records.

Cemetery in Arneytown, New Jersey. His devoted Emily passed away on August 2014 and is buried there as well.

Andrew's grandson (the author) continued his Navy tradition by serving as a Navy Reserve Religious Program Specialist (Fleet Marine Force). He mobilized and deployed twice for Operation Iraqi Freedom.

Conclusion

For nearly thirty years, she sailed under three different names for four different owners. She underwent three major reconstructions which converted her from a passenger / cargo liner to an escort aircraft carrier and back to a passenger / cargo liner. During World War II, she trained thousands of U.S. Navy carrier pilots for war and significantly contributed to the Allied victory over Nazi Germany and Imperial Japan. Her wartime crew included a future Vice Admiral, a famed fighter pilot and my grandfather. After the war, she transported tens of thousands of war refugees to start new lives in Australia and New Zealand. During her time, *Charger* sailed across the globe performing a wide variety of missions.

USS Charger Photo Album
(All photos from U.S. Naval History and Heritage Command except where noted)

USS Charger underway. (National Archives photo)

Charger at anchor 12 May 1942. She is adorned in Camouflage Pattern 12 (Modified).

F4F-4 Wildcats stowed on *Charger*'s Hangar Deck on 2 October 1942, prior to departure for Bermuda.

Flight operations aboard *USS Charger* in May 1944.

Avenger bomber comes in for a landing aboard *USS Charger* on
22 April 1944. The Avenger is part of either Torpedo Squadron
Three Hundred One (VT-301) or Torpedo Squadron Thirteen
(VT-13), both of which qualified pilots that day.

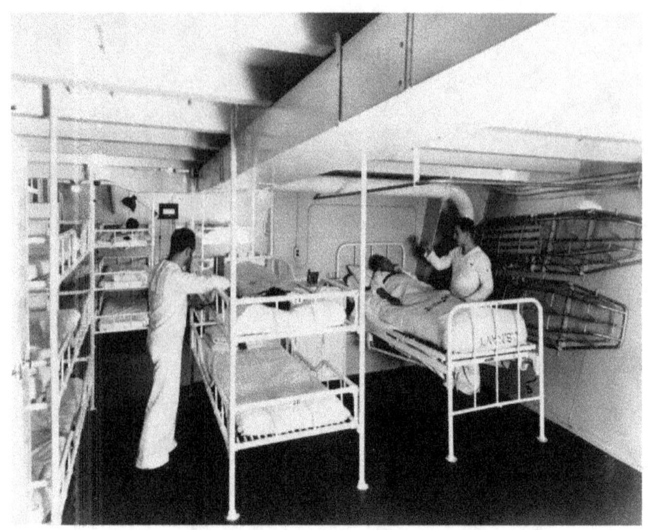

Navy Corpsmen treat patients in *Charger*'s Sick Bay
(August 1942)

Worship services are held on *Charger*'s Hangar Deck on Sunday
17 December 1944. Among those in attendance are a group of
female U.S. Coast Guard members (SPARS).

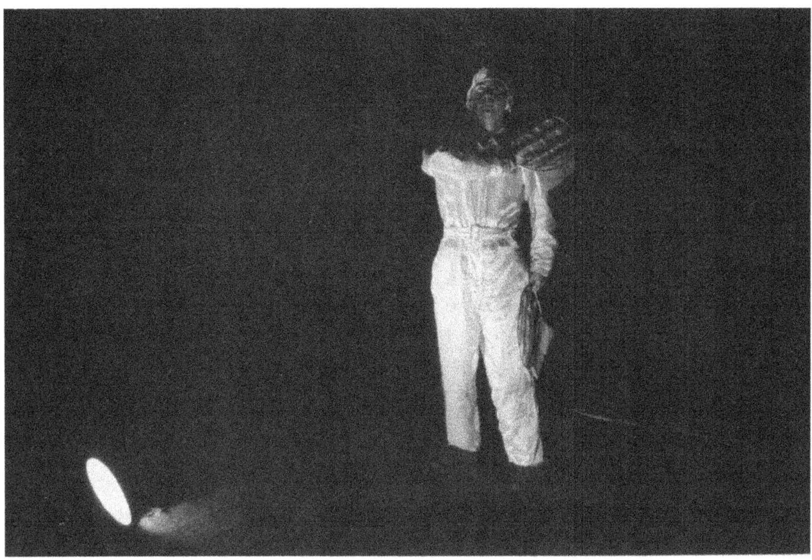

Assistant LSO ENS Ralph Thibodeau demonstrates the new High Visibility LSO Suit (6 September 1944).

ENS Ralph Thibodeau climbs into a SNJ on the deck of *USS Charger.* (Photo courtesy of Ralph Thibodeau Jr.).

CAPT Thomas L. Sprague, USN,
first commanding officer of *USS Charger.*

In October 1942, *USS Charger* steamed to Bermuda with *USS Ranger* (CV-4) (above) for Operation Torch. At the last minute, *Charger* was replaced by *USS Suwanee* (CVE-27) (below). *Charger* returned to Norfolk to resume training carrier pilots.

ENS Ralph Thibodeau (Photo Courtesy of Ralph Thibodeau Jr).

Andrew S. Futey, USNR
(Futey Family Photo)

Andrew S. Futey Recruit Graduation Photo
(Futey Family Photo)

APPENDIX A
SQUADRONS KNOWN TO HAVE TRAINED
ABOARD *USS CHARGER*

NACTU 211		NOV 1945
VB-15	SB2C Helldivers	OCT 1944
VB-16	SB2C Helldivers	JAN 1945
VB-75	SB2C Helldivers	SEP 1945
VB-80	SB2C Helldivers	APR / MAY 1944
VB-82	SB2C Helldivers	JUN / JUL 1944, SEP 1944
VB-85	SB2C Helldivers	AUG 1944
VB-87	SB2C Helldivers	OCT 1944
VB-89	SB2C Helldivers	JAN / FEB 1945
VB-95	SB2C Helldivers	MAR 1945
VBF-20	F4U Corsairs	JUL 1945
VBF-89	F6F Hellcats	JAN / FEB 1945, APR 1945
VBF-93	F4U Corsairs	JUL 1945
VBF-94	F4U Corsairs	MAR / APR 1945
VBF-95	F4U Corsairs	MAR / APR 1945
VBF-150	F4U Corsairs	MAR / APR 1945
VBF-151	F4U Corsairs	APR 1945
VBF-152	FG1 / F4U Corsairs	JUL 1945
VBF-153	FG1 / F4U Corsairs	JUL 1945
VC-6	TBM Avengers	APR / MAY 1944, FEB 1945
VC-8	TBM Avengers	MAY 1944, AUG / SEP 1944
	FM-2 Wildcats	

VC-12	TBM Avengers	MAY / JUN 1944, OCT 1944
	FM-2 Wildcats	
VC-13	FM-2 Wildcats	JUN 1944
	TBM Avengers	
VC-15	FM2 Wildcats	APR 1944, JAN / FEB /
	TBM Avengers	MAR / APR 1945
VC-19	FM-2 Wildcats	JUN / JUL 1944, APR 1945
	TBM Avengers	
VC-36	TBF Avengers	AUG 1944
VC-55	F4F Wildcats	APR 1944, SEP / OCT 1944,
	TBF Avengers	MAR 1945
VC-58	TBF-1 Avengers	JUN 1944
VC-69		APR / MAY 1944, SEP 1944
VC-80	FM-2 Wildcats	APR 1944
	TBM Avengers	
VC-95	FM-2 Wildcats	OCT 1944
	TBF Avengers	
VF-16	F6F Hellcats	JAN 1945
VF-17	F4U Corsairs	MAR 1943
VF-27	F6F Hellcats	APR 1945
VF-74	F6F Hellcats	APR 1944
VF-80	F6F-3 Hellcats	APR 1944
VF-82	F6F-3 Hellcats	JUN / JUL / AUG / SEP 1944
VF-86	F6F Hellcats	AUG / SEP 1944
VF-87	F6F Hellcats	OCT 1944
VF-89	F6F Hellcats	FEB / MAR / APR 1945

VF-94	F6F Hellcats	MAR 1945
VF-95	F6F Hellcats	MAR 1945
	FG-1 Corsairs	
VF-153	F6F Hellcats	JUL 1945
VFN-78	F6F-5N Hellcats	MAY 1944
VFN-79	F6F-5N Hellcats	MAY 1944
VGF-29	F4F Wildcats	AUG 1942
VGS-30	F4F Wildcats	APR 1942
VOF-1	F6F Hellcats	APR 1944
	TBF Avengers	
VOF-2	F4U Corsairs	APR / MAY 1944
VT-13	TBF Avengers	APR 1944
VT-16	TBM Avengers	JAN 1945
VT-20	TBF Avengers	JUL 1945
VT-43	TBM Avengers	NOV 1945
VT-75	TBM Avengers	SEP 1945, OCT 1945
VT-82	TBM Avengers	JUN / JUL 1944, SEP 1944
VT-87	TBF Avengers	OCT 1944
VT-89	TBM Avengers	JAN / FEB / MAR 1945
VT-95	TBF Avengers	OCT 1944
VT-301	TBF Avengers	APR 1944
No. 738 (RN)	F4U Corsairs	APR 1944, AUG 1944
		FEB / MAR 1945,
No. 841 (RN)	F4U Corsairs	MAY 1944
No. 856 (RN)	F4U Corsairs	APR 1944

No. 1552 (RN) F4U Corsairs   APR 1945

No. 1820 (RN) F4U Corsairs   JUN 1944

No. 1835 (RN) F4U Corsairs   FEB / MAR 1945

No. 1841 (RN) F4U Corsairs   MAY 1944

No. 1842 (RN) F4U Corsairs   JUN 1944

No. 1843 (RN) F4U Corsairs   JUN 1944

No. 1846 (RN) F4U Corsairs   AUG 1944

No. 1848 (RN) F4U Corsairs   AUG 1944

No. 1849 (RN) F4U Corsairs   OCT 1944

No. 1850 (RN) F4U Corsairs   SEP 1944

RN: Royal Navy
VB: Bombing Squadron
VBF: Bombing / Fighting Squadron
VC: Fleet Composite Squadron
VF: Fighting Squadron
VFN: Night Fighting Squadron
VGF: Auxiliary Fighting Squadron
VGS: Auxiliary Scouting Squadron
VOF: Observation Fighting Squadron
VT: Torpedo Squadron
[In 1943, VGF and VGS squadrons were re-designated as Fleet Composite Squadrons (VC).]

APPENDIX B
SQUADRONS KNOWN TO HAVE TRAINED ABOARD *USS CHARGER* BY MONTH

APR 1942   VGS-30

AUG 1942   VGF-29

MAR 1943   VF-17

DEC 1943
VC-15	VF-9	VF-50
VC-36	VF-14	VF-51
VC-58	VF-15	VFW-76
VC-196	VF(N)-75	VN-15
No. 852 (RN)		

FEB 1944
VF-13	VB-13	VT-13
VC-6	VC-95	

MAR 1944
VC-19	VF-7	VOF-1
VC-58	VT-19	VF-51
VC-84	VC-36	No. 855 RN
No. 732 RN	No. 852 RN	

APR 1944
VOF-1	VC-55	VC-19
VOF-2	VB-80	VT-301
VF-74	VC-15	VT-13
VF-80	VC-80	VC-69
No. 738 (RN)	VC-6	No. 856 (RN)

MAY 1944	VOF-2	VC-6	VC-69
	VC-8	VC-12	VFN-78
	VFN-79	VB-80	No. 841 (RN)
	No. 1841 (RN)		

JUN 1944	VC-12	VC-13	VC-19
	VC-58	VB-82	VF-82
	VT-82		No. 1820 (RN)
	No. 1842 (RN)		No. 1843 (RN)

JUL 1944	VC-19	VB-82	VF-82
	VT-82		

AUG 1944	VB-86	VC-8	VC-36
	VF-82	VF-86	No. 738 (RN)
	No. 1846 (RN)		No. 1848 (RN)

SEP 1944	VB-82	VC-8	VC-55
	VC-69	VF-82	VF-86
	VT-82	No. 1850 (RN)	

OCT 1944	VC-55	VC-95	VT-95
	VB-15	VF-87	VC-12
	VB-87	VT-87	No. 1849 (RN)

NOV 1944	VB-85	VC-15	VF-16
	VC-9	VC-19	VF-85
	VC-12	VF-87	No. 1851 (RN)

DEC 1944	VB-16	VT-16	VC-15
	VF-16	VC-8	VC-13
	No. 83 (RN)		
JAN 1945	VT-89	VBF-89	VT-16
	VF-16	VC-15	VB-89
	VB-16		
FEB 1945	VT-89	VB-89	VBF-89
	VF-89	VC-6	VC-15
	No. 738 (RN)		No. 1835 (RN)
MAR 1945	VC-15	VBF-94	VT-89
	VF-89	VB-95	VBF-95
	VC-55	VF-94	VF-95
	VBF-150	No. 738 (RN)	
	No. 1835 (RN)		
APR 1945	VBF-89	VC-15	VF-89
	VBF-94	VBF-95	VBF-150
	VC-19	VF-27	VBF-151
	No. 1552 (RN)		
May 1945	VB-151	VBF-89	VBF-93
	VBF-95	VBF-150	VBF-151
	VBF-181	VC-15	VC-95
	VF-28	VF-93	VF-95
	VT-95	VT-150	No. 738 (RN)

JUL 1945   VBF-20   VBF-93   VBF-153
                  VF-153   VT-20

SEP 1945   VB-75   VT-75

OCT 1945   VT-75

NOV 1945   VT-43   VBF-20   VT-43
                  NACTU 211   VF-43   VF-81
                  VBF-81

RN: Royal Navy
VB: Bombing Squadron
VBF: Bombing / Fighting Squadron
VC: Fleet Composite Squadron
VF: Fighting Squadron
VFN: Night Fighting Squadron
VGS: Auxiliary Scouting Squadron
VOF: Observation Fighting Squadron
VT: Torpedo Squadron

APPENDIX C -
MILESTONE CARRIER LANDINGS
(Source: *History of U.S.S. Charger (CVE-30)*, 24 May 1945)

1st	27 April 1942	LT C. W. Stewart
1st (trainee)	27 April 1942	ENS Kelly (VGS-30)
1,000th	4 July 1942	
2,000th	9 August 1942	
3,000th	10 November 1942	
4,000th	15 December 1942	
5,000th	3 January 1943	
6,000th	17 January 1943	
7,000th	13 February 1943	
8,000th	4 March 1943	
9,000th	16 March 1943	
10,000th	28 March 1943	ENS E. Delanez
11,000th	22 April 1943	
12,000th	14 May 1943	
13,000th	15 June 1943	
14,000th	14 August 1943	
1st Night Landing	10 September 1943	LCDR Avery
15,000th	10 September 1943	
16,000th	6 October 1943	ENS R. H. Zehgen
		SBD Dauntless
17,000th	1 November 1943	
18,000th	22 November 1943	
19,000th	17 December 1943	
20,000th	4 February 1944	
21,000th	5 March 1944	

22,000th   5 April 1944

23,000th   20 April 1944

24,000th   8 May 1944

25,000th   20 June 1944   ENS Pfeifer (VF-82)

26,000th   1 July 1944

27,000th   21 July 1944

28,000th   7 August 1944

29,000th   23 August 1944

30,000th   10 October 1944   LT(jg) H. P. Brehm (VF-87)

31,000th   15 October 1944

32,000th   28 October 1944   LT(jg) S. M. Tridman (VF-87)

33,000th   11 November 1944

34,000th   15 December 1944

35,000th   29 December 1944

36,000th

37,000th   18 January 1945

38,000th   18 February 1945

39,000th   9 March 1945

40,000th   21 March 1945

41,000th   29 March 1945

42,000th   5 April 1945

43,000th   18 April 1945

44,000th   30 April 1945

50,000th   29 November 1945   ENS Robert A. Scott (VT-43)

Most Landings (Month) 2,500   September 1944
Most Day Landings (Day) 404   15 September 1944

APPENDIX D -
COMMANDING OFFICERS &
EXECUTIVE OFFICERS

Commanding Officers

CAPT Thomas L. Sprague   Commissioning to 15 DEC 1942

CAPT Grover B. H. Hall   15 DEC 1942 to 6 NOV 1943

CAPT Ralph W. D. Woods   6 NOV 1943 to 26 AUG 1944

CAPT Robert Ruffin Johnson   26 AUG 1944 to 5 JUL 1945

CAPT William M. Walsh   5 JUL 1945 to Decommissioning

Executive Officers

CDR Steven W. Calloway

CDR Charles Loomis Lee

CDR Thomas Andrew Ahroon

CDR Lawrence Oldham Matthews Jr.

CDR Warren Roland Thompson

CDR Keith Eikenberger Taylor

Appendix E

USS Charger Memorial Roll

Training for war can be just as deadly as war itself. The following pilots lost their lives while conducting training in conjuction with *USS Charger* in the Chesapeake Bay.

ENS F. G. Barnes	VGF-29	8 August 1942
ENS Gordon G. Behrens		12 January 1943
ENS Ivan Acton Edwards		5 November 1943
ENS John A. Hafner	VBF-150	31 March 1945
ENS Leon J. Laurin	VB-87	27 October 1944
ENS Maurice J. Lambert	VC-15	Date Unknown
LT(jg) W. R. Livegey		10 April 1943
ENS Daniel Francis Malloy Jr.	VB-151	21 May 1945

SOURCES

National Archives
The sources in this section are official U.S. Navy records preserved by the National Archives II, College Park, Maryland. They are organized as part of Record Group 38. Many of these records are also available in digital format from www.fold3.com

Major Commands
U.S. Navy. Atlantic Fleet. Carriers, Atlantic Fleet. War Diary for Period 1 October 1942 to 23 October 1942. 23 October 1942.

U.S. Navy. Atlantic Fleet. Fleet Air Command, Norfolk. War Diary. January 1944.

U.S. Navy. Bureau of Aeronautics. Interview of CAPT J. J. Clark, USN. *USS Suwannee.* In the Bureau of Aeronautics 27 November 1942.

U.S. Navy. Naval Operating Base Bermuda. War Diary for October 1942.

U.S. Navy Pre-Flight School. St. Mary's College, California. War Diary 1 to 30 November 1945.

Ships
USS Ellyson (DD-454). War Diary. October 1942.

USS Suwannee (ACV-27). War Diary. September 24, 1942 to November 1, 1942.

U.S. Navy Aviation Squadrons

Air Group Seventy-Five. Torpedo Squadron Seventy-Five.
War Diary for September 1945. 1 October 1945.

Auxiliary Scouting Squadron Thirty (VGS-30). War Diary.
April 1942.

Auxiliary Scouting Squadron Thirty (VGS-30). War Diary.
May 1942.

Bombing Squadron Fifteen. War History. Undated.

Bombing Squadron Sixteen. War Diary 1 Dec 44 to 31 Dec 44.
1 January 1945.

Bombing Squadron Eighty-Six. War Diary September 1944.
30 September 1944.

Bombing Squadron Eighty-Six. War History. Undated.

Bombing Squadron Eighty-Seven. War Diary for October 1944.
4 November 1944.

Bombing Squadron Eighty-Seven. History of Bombing Squadron
Eighty-Seven. Undated.

Bombing Squadron Eighty-Nine. War History. 23 April 1946.

Bombing Squadron One Hundred Fifty-One. War Diary for
May 1945. 1 June 1945.

Bombing Fighting Squadron One Hundred Fifty. War Diary
1 March to 31 March 1945. 2 April 1945.

Bombing Fighting Squadron One Hundred Fifty. War Diary.
1 May to 31 May 1945. 1 June 1945.

Bombing Fighting Squadron One Hundred Fifty-One. War Diary.
Month of April 1945. 3 May 1945.

Bombing Fighting Squadron One Hundred Fifty-Three. War Diary.
June 1945. 1 July 1945.

Composite Squadron Fifteen. VC-15. History of Composite
Squadron 15. Undated.

Escort Fighting Squadron Twenty-Nine. VGF-29. War Diary.
18 July 1942 to 31 October 1942.

Fighting Squadron Twenty-Seven. History of Fighting Squadron
Twenty-Seven 15 October 1943 - 1 March 1945.

Fighting Squadron Twenty-Seven. History of Fighting Squadron
Twenty-Seven. 26 October 1945.

Fighting Squadron Eighty. History of Fighting Squadron Eighty.
6 September 1944.

Fighting Squadron Eighty-Seven. War Diary for October 1944.
4 November 1944.

Fighting Squadron One Hundred Fifty-Three. War Diary.
June 1945. 1 July 1945.

Torpedo Squadron Eighty-Nine. War Diary for January 1945.
1 February 1945.

Torpedo Squadron One Hundred Fifty. War Diary for May 1945.

U.S. Navy. Pacific Fleet. Air Forces, Pacific Fleet. Fighting
   Squadron Eighty-Seven. War History. 20 October 1945.

USS Charger **(CVE-30)**

USS Charger. CVE-30 History of *USS Charger* (CVE-30).
   24 May 1945.

USS Charger. CVE-30. War Diary for March 1942.

USS Charger. CVE-30. War Diary for April 1942.

USS Charger. CVE-30 War Diary for May 1942.

USS Charger. (CVE-30). War Diary for the Month of October
   1942.

USS Charger. (CVE-30). War Diary for the Month of November
   1942.

USS Charger. CVE-30. Deck Log. December 1942.

USS Charger. CVE-30. Deck Log. January 1943.

USS Charger. CVE-30. Deck Log. February 1943.

USS Charger. CVE-30. Deck Log. March 1943.

USS Charger. CVE-30. Deck Log. April 1943.

USS Charger. CVE-30. Deck Log. May 1943.

USS Charger. CVE-30. Deck Log. June 1943.

USS Charger. CVE-30. Deck Log. July 1943.

USS Charger. CVE-30.   Deck Log. August 1943.

USS Charger. CVE-30.   Deck Log.   September 1943.

USS Charger. CVE-30.   Deck Log.   October 1943.

USS Charger. CVE-30.   Deck Log. November 1943.

USS Charger. CVE-30.   War Diary for December 1943.
   1 January 1944.

USS Charger. CVE-30. War Diary 1 FEB 1944 to 29 FEB 1944.
   10 March 1944.

USS Charger. CVE-30.   War Diary. 1 March to 31 March 1944.
   3 April 1944.

USS Charger. CVE-30 War Diary for April 1944. 1 May 1944.

USS Charger. CVE-30 War Diary for May 1944. 1 June 1944.

USS Charger. CVE-30 War Diary for June 1944. 3 July 1944.

USS Charger. CVE-30 War Diary for July 1944. 8 August 1944.

USS Charger. CVE-30 War Diary for August 1944. 1 September
   1944.

USS Charger. CVE-30 War Diary for September 1944. 1 October
   1944.

USS Charger. CVE-30 War Diary for October 1944. 1 November
   1944.

USS Charger. CVE-30 War Diary for November 1944.
1 December 1944.

USS Charger. CVE-30 War Diary for December 1944. 1 January
1945.

USS Charger. CVE-30 War Diary for January 1945. 1 February
1945.

USS Charger. CVE-30 War Diary for February 1945. 1 March
1945.

USS Charger. CVE-30 War Diary for March 1945. 1 April 1945.

USS Charger. CVE-30 War Diary for April 1945. 1 May 1945.

USS Charger. CVE-30. War Diary May 1945. 1 June 1945.

USS Charger. CVE-30 War Diary for July 1945. 1 August 1945.

USS Charger. CVE-30 War Diary for August 1945. 1 September
1945.

USS Charger (CVE-30). War Diary for September 1945.
1 October 1945

USS *Charger* (CVE-30). War Diary 1 OCT 1945 to 31 OCT 1945.
1 November 1945.

USS Charger (CVE-30). War Diary 1 NOV 1945 to 30 NOV
1945. 1 December 1945.

USS Charger. (CVE-30). War Diary 1 December 1945 to 31
December 1945. 1 January 1946.

Primary Sources

Blackburn, Tom and Eric Hammel, *The Jolly Rogers: The Story of Tom Blackburn and Navy Fighting Squadron VF-17*. St. Paul, MN: Zenith P, 1998).

"Catapult-Fire!" *Naval Aviation News*. August 1946: pp.18-24.

"Ensign John F. Darcy." *Democrat and Chronicle* (Rochester, NY). May 30, 1945: pg. 7.

Falat, John. "Petition for Citizenship." Accepted by U.S. District Court of the Southern District of New York. June 16, 1932. Photo-copy in possession of author.

Thibodeau, Ralph A., Jr. "Ralph A. Thibodeau." Unpublished biography. August 2020.

Trangmar, Paul. Email to the Author. 19 March 2019.

U.S. Geological Survey. "Marcus Hook, P.A. - DEL. - N.J." Topographical Map, 1941.

U.S. Navy. Commander, Navy Region Southeast. Naval Station Guantanamo Bay. History. Accessed online on 15 June 2020 at https://www.cnic.navy.mil/regions/cnrse/installations/ ns_guantanamo_bay/about/history.html

U.S. Navy. Office of Information. Biographies Branch. "Rear Admiral Thomas A. Ahroon – United States Navy." 31 March 1960.

U.S. Navy. United States Fleet. Commander in Chief, United
States Fleet, and Chief of Naval Operations. Fleet Admiral
Ernest J. King, USN. *First Report to the Secretary of the Navy.*
23 April 1944. Accessed on 17 April 2020 at http://
www.ibiblio.org/hyperwar/USN/USNatWar/USN-King-1.html

U.S. Navy. *USS Charger.* CVE-30. *The Super Charger.*
Christmas Issue 1944. Copy courtesy of Ralph Thibodeau Jr.

Secondary Sources

Algeria-French Morocco. In the series *The U.S. Army Campaigns
of World War II.* CMH Publication 72-11. Washington DC:
U.S. Army Center of Military History, 1995.

Germinsky, Robert A., CE1, USNR. "A Brief History of U.S.
Navy Aircraft Carriers - The Escort Carriers." 15 June 2009.
Accessed online on 21 April 2020 at
https://www.navy.mil/navydata/nav_legacy.asp?id=3

Hanna, Ira R.   ""One Century Ago: Naval Air Station Norfolk's
First Skipper, Part 1: P.N.L. Bellinger: Pioneer Naval Aviator
and the Early Days of NAS Norfolk." Hampton Roads Naval
Museum Blog. August 27, 2018. Accessed online on 9 June
2020 at https://hamptonroadsnavalmuseum.blogspot.com/
search?q=bellinger
___________. "One Century Ago: Naval Air Station Norfolk's
First Skipper, Part 2." Hampton Roads Naval Museum Blog.
September 21, 2018. Accessed online on 9 June 2020 at
https://hamptonroadsnavalmuseum.blogspot.com/2018/09/one-
century-ago-naval-air-station.html

Hutchinson, Robert. *Jane's Warship Recognition Guide.* London:
HarperCollins, 2002.

Kavanagh, Dave, et. als. "Sun Shipbuilding and Drydock
    Company Hull Listing." Prepared by the Sun Ship Historical
    Society. 9 March 2004.

MacDonald, Scot. *Evolution of Aircraft Carriers.* Washington DC
    GPO: Office of the Chief of Naval Operations, 1962.

McIntyre, Donald, Captain RN (Ret.), *Aircraft Carrier – The
    Majestic Weapon.* NY: Ballantine, 1968.

Moore, John, Captain, Royal Navy. *Jane's American Fighting
    Ships of the 20th Century.* NY: Mallard P, 1991.

Morison, Samuel Eliot. *History of United States Naval Operations
    in World War II. Volume II - Operations in North African
    Waters: October 1942 to June 1943.* Boston: Brown, Little &
    Co., 1947.
    ___________________. *History of United States Naval Operations
    in World War II. Volume X The Atlantic Battle Won May 1943
    – May 1945.* Boston: Brown, Little & Co., 1956.
    ___________________. *History of United States Naval Operations
    in World War II. Volume XII - Leyte June 1944 - January 1945.*
    Boston: Little, Brown & Co., 1958.
    ___________________. *History of United States Naval
    Operations in World War II. Volume XIV - Victory in the Pacific.*
    Boston: Little, Brown & Co., 1960.

Museum Victoria (Australia.) "Post World War II Immigrant
    Ships: Fairsea." Museum Victoria Fact Sheet (2007). Found
    online at http://museumvictoria.com.au/DiscoveryCentre/
Infosheets/Fairsea/

U.S. Naval History and Heritage Command. "Jesse Barrett
     Oldendorf   16 February 1887 - 27 April 1974."   Accessed
     online on 10 September 2020 at https://www.history.navy.mil/
research/library/research-guides/modern-biographical-files-ndl/
modern-bios-o/oldendorf-jesse-barrett.html
______________________________________. "Patrick Nieson
     Lynch Bellinger   8 October 1885 - 29 May 1962."
     Accessed on 9 June 2020 at https://www.history.navy.mil/
research/library/research-guides/modern-biographical-files-ndl/
modern-bios-b/bellinger-patrick-n.html

Websites
Tony Drury. http://www.royalnavyresearcharchive.org.uk/
ESCORT/

NTS Sampson Museum. www.rpadden.com/sampson.htm.

Ralph W. D. Woods Veteran Tribute http://
www.veterantributes.org/TributeDetail.php?recordID=990

Sun Shipbuilding Historical Society. www.sunship.org

ABOUT THE AUTHOR

Bryan J. Dickerson is a military and naval historian specializing in World War II. He holds a Bachelor's of Arts degree in History from Rowan University and a Master's of Arts degree in American History from Monmouth University. A former U.S. Navy Reserve Religious Program Specialist 1st Class (Fleet Marine Force), he mobilized and deployed twice to Iraq for Operation Iraqi Freedom. He is a Fourth Degree member of the Knights of Columbus Catholic Men's Service Organization and a Past Grand Knight. He is the author of fifteen books and numerous online and print articles. He, his wife Lisa and their children live in Gloucester County, New Jersey.

Other Books by Bryan J. Dickerson

The Liberators of Pilsen: The U.S. Army 16th Armored Division in World War Two Czechoslovakia

*Marine General from the Ranks:
The Life of Lt Gen Homer L. Litzenberg Jr.*

Modern Saints and Blesseds of the Catholic Church

The Organized Marine Corps Reserve in World War Two

An Anthology of Military and Cold War History

History of Marine Wing Support Squadron 472

*To The Fallen: A Centenarian Remembrance of
the First World War*

Works in Progress

Plane Spotting Around Philadelphia

War and Peace in the South China Sea

The End of the End Times

The End of the End Times 2.0

Modern Saints and Blesseds of the Catholic Church Volume 2

A Love That Never Was

www.ingramcontent.com/pod-product-compliance
Lightning Source LLC
Chambersburg PA
CBHW072226150726
48002CB00005B/1961